Lifelines 1

COPING SKILLS IN ENGLISH

SECOND EDITION

Barbara Foley

Howard Pomann

PRENTICE HALL REGENTS

This series is dedicated to our dear friend and colleague, Gretchen Dowling.

Gretchen Dowling
8/31/43 – 4/13/89

Acquisitions Editor: Anne Riddick
Production Supervision: Kala Dwarakanath
   and Noël Vreeland Carter
Interior Design: A Good Thing
   and Jerry Votta
Cover Design: Jerry Votta
Prepress Buyer: Ray Keating
Manufacturing Buyer: Lori Bulwin
Scheduler: Leslie Coward

Photo Credits:
Abraham Feria, Units 1, 2, 10, 16; Laima Druskis Units 3, 4, 6; Mike Mazzaschi/Stock, Boston, Unit 5; Rafael Macia/Photo Researchers, Unit 7; Marc Anderson, Units 8, 13; Ken Karp, Units 9, 14; Mimi Forsyth/Monkmeyer Press, Unit 11; Matusou/Monkmeyer Press, Unit 12; Courtesy of IBM; Unit 15; Spencer Grant/Monkmeyer Press, Unit 18; Philip Bailey, Unit 19; Courtesy of A.T. & T.

1992 by Prentice Hall Regents

Printed in the United States of America
20 19 18 17 16 15 14 13 12 11

0-13-529538-6

Contents

Introduction

Barbara Foley and Howard Pomann have devised this survival skills series specifically for entry-level adult students who need to learn basic skills and basic language in order to function effectively in the United States. The conversations and practices lead students through carefully controlled exercises to the point where they can "put it together" for themselves. In addition to whole-class and large-group activities, LIFELINES features many small-group activities which allow the teacher to step aside and become a facilitator as the students work together using the language in new and different ways. The focus on coping skills and functional language, rather than grammar and vocabulary, promotes learning by increasing student interest. The repetition of the same basic exercise formats throughout, allows students to concentrate on learning language, not exercise formats. Gretchen Dowling's excellent "To the Teacher" section gives clear explanations of how to do each exercise, along with an abundance of ideas for adapting them to your own individual needs. Photographs, drawings and realia bring the content of each unit to life for students. LIFELINES really makes learning easier for your students, and teaching easier for you.

Sharon Seymour
Alemany Community
College Center
San Francisco

To the Teacher

Lifelines is a four-book ESL coping skills series for adult learners at entry, beginning, low-intermediate and intermediate levels. Each book deals with ten or more different coping skill areas. The series is competency-based and integrates the coping skills with the essential language forms, vocabulary, and cultural information needed in each situation.

Skill areas are reintroduced throughout the series with different competencies. For example, in "Telephone," in Book 1, students ask to speak with someone; in Book 2, they leave a simple message; in Book 3, they give and take a longer message; in Book 4, they ask for the right person or office. Those competencies requiring simpler language forms come before those calling for more difficult ones. Thus, grammatical points such as verb tenses are introduced in appropriate sequence. They are reintroduced cyclically throughout the series and via the different contexts within each book.

The series is suitable for a wide variety of adult and secondary school clases. It could be the total program, for example, for open-entry ESL classes of 3-6 hours per week. For intensive language courses, it would probably be one strand of the total program. In community college or secondary school classes, it could be used either to reinforce grammatical structures, or to introduce them in context.

Each unit is self-contained, takes approximately two hours, and affords practice in listening, speaking, reading, and writing. The table of contents for each book lists the coping skill areas, the functions or competencies, and the main grammatical structures in each chapter. This gives the teacher easy access to the information needed to choose how best to integrate LIFELINES with individual programs, classes, and teaching styles.

The series incorporates both whole class and small group learning activities. All the activities are designed to give students as much "inner space" as possible to process the language according to their own individual learning styles. Those for the whole class are to introduce or sum up the structure, vocabulary, and cultural information needed to perform the coping skill; those for the small groups, to provide students with the intensive independent practice they need to make the language their own.

In the whole class activities, the teacher utilizes stories, pictures, and conversations to introduce the new language and information in the chapter. Although the teacher is leading the activity, the activities are designed so that the teacher can easily elicit the correct language with minimal teacher modeling.

In small group activities, the teacher's role is that of a small group facilitator assisting the students in completing their tasks, rather than that of a leader. Depending on the activity and level of the students, a teacher can circulate from group to group, stay with one group, or sit separately from the groups and assist only when asked.

Students working in small groups learn to discover their own mistakes, to correct each other, to share opinions, to experiment with the language, and to work as a learning community. Small groups allow the teacher to divide the class according to particular language needs, and to work with students having individual problems as well as those who are ahead of the class. They also free students to ask questions they may not ask in the whole class setting.

For the teacher, one of the biggest advantages of LIFELINES is that small group work, and accommodation to different learning styles, are built-in. It is not necessary to supplement the books with small group tasks in order to meet individual student needs. The small group activities have been tested with a wide variety of students. They work without extra work for the teacher.

Naturally, there are many ways to handle the activities presented in the workbooks, depending on students' proficiency levels, and the teacher's personal style. In the pages which follow, the authors offer "how to" suggestions which have proven effective for them. These are intended simply as some ways to structure classwork so that students have maximum opportunity to meet their own learning needs in a productive and secure atmosphere. They are not intended as limits on the readers' style or creativity.

WHOLE CLASS ACTIVITIES

Discuss

Discuss
The Discuss questions and accompanying illustration or photo set the scene for the unit. The class should talk about the illustration and what they see happening in the picture. The Discuss questions help the student to relate their personal opinions and experiences to the theme of the unit. Cultural comments and explanations can be made at this time. During this introduction to the unit, the focus is on expanding the students' knowledge of the coping skill rather than the correction of grammar.

Listen, Read and Say

Listen, Read and Say
This is the dialog which introduces the language and competency. It is the core from which all the other activities and expansions in the chapter emerge. Thus, it is vital that the meaning be clear to the students.

Step 1: Students read the dialog to themselves and figure out as much of the meaning as they can on their own. During this process, they can talk to each other and even translate. The surer they are that they know what the dialog says in their own language, the easier it is for them to "let go" and absorb the English. The teacher can circulate, answering individual questions and/or getting a sense of what may be needed to explain to the entire group.

Step 2: When students feel reasonably clear about the meaning, the teacher makes any necessary further clarification, dramatizations, or explanations. The teacher may then want to read the dialog aloud once or twice while students listen and look at their books. This helps them associate the sound of English with the meanings they have worked out. The dialog may be written on the board and the students asked to close their books. This serves as a signal to focus on English together.

Step 3: Practice the dialog. (a) This can be done by the usual choral then individual repetition, followed by half the class taking one speaker's part while half takes the other, culminating with individual students role playing the parts.

(b) A variation or supplement to this is to change the "rules of the game" and have the teacher repeat after the students. The teacher stands at the back of the room, and lets the students, one at a time, call out whatever word, phrase or sentence they want to hear. The teacher repeats the student's utterance until the student stops initiating the repetition. The teacher behaves like a tape recorder with a natural, non-judgemental voice: by just letting the students hear the utterance they "ask" for, the exercise helps them self-correct and develop their own criteria for grammar and pronunciation. If students fail to self-correct an important point, it is best to deal with the point after the exercise, rather than to break the mood of the self-directed learning.

Since this exercise is a bit different from what most classes are accustomed to, it is necessary to explain it clearly beforehand. With very basic classes to whom one cannot translate, it often helps to number the sentences in the dialog. Then the teacher can say and easily demonstrate, "Tell me the number you want to hear. I will say the sentence. If you say the number again, I will repeat the sentence. I am a machine. I will repeat what you say. I will stop when you say 'stop'."

(c) As an aid to internalizing the dialog, the teacher can erase every fifth word and replace it with a line, having students read the dialog while orally filling in the missing words. This procedure is repeated with lines for every third word, and so on, until students are "reading" a dialog composed of completely blank lines. Members of the class might then cooperate in filling in all the blanks to reinforce correct spelling, etc.

Practice

This activity introduces new vocabulary within the previously established context and grammatical structures. A single sentence or interaction from the dialog is given as the model. Students practice the model, substituting the vocabulary cued by the pictures below it.

Step 1: If much of the vocabulary is new, students can repeat each item in isolation, chorally and then individually, following the teacher's model.

Step 2: The teacher elicits the use of the new items within the model sentence or interaction. One way to do this is simply to have the students repeat the complete utterances after the teacher. This is a good first step, especially for very low-level classes. After this initial security is given, however, students need a little more independence.

A variation, or follow-up, is for the teacher to give only the first utterance as a model. The teacher then simply points to or calls out the number of each different picture and has the students give the complete utterance. This can be done both chorally and individually.

Step 3: Students can then continue practicing all the substitutions, with the person sitting next to them. The teacher can circulate, helping with pronunciation as necessary.

Step 4: To further reinforce the pronunciation of the new vocabulary, follow the procedures described in Step 4b of Listen, Read, and Say.

SMALL GROUP ACTIVITIES

Before beginning the small group activities, the teacher divides the students in groups of two to five depending on the activity and the size of the class. The teacher then goes over the directions carefully and demonstrates what each student will do, explaining what the teacher's role will be, whether circulating from group to group, or staying with one group. The teacher should give the students a time frame; for example, telling the students they have fifteen minutes to complete the task. The time frame can always be extended. Clear information about what to expect helps students feel secure and be more productive.

There are many different ways to group students. Some teachers like to have students of the same ability together; others to mix them so the more advanced can help the slower. Some like to mix language backgrounds in order to encourage the use of English; others to have the same backgrounds together in order to raise the security level, or to facilitate students' explaining things to each other. Some like student self-selection so that working friendships may develop more easily; others don't see this as crucial to the development of supportive, productive groups. Each teacher's values and pedagogical purposes will determine the way the class is divided into groups.

Partner Exercise

Partner Exercise

This small-group activity is designed for two students to practice a specific grammatical structure in a controlled interaction. The left-hand column of the *Partner Exercise* gives word or picture cues from which Student 1 forms a statement or question. The right-hand column gives the complete sentences. Student 2 looks at this column, using it to be "teacher" and check the utterances of the other student. Students are to fold the page in the middle so that S1 is looking at the left-hand column and S2 at the right.

Step 1: The teacher explains all this to the students. One way is to copy two or three items in the left-hand column on one side of the board. (It is not necessary to worry about awkward picture drawing; it usually just provides a few moments of laughter for the class.)

(b) Then draw the corresponding items from the right-hand column on the other side of the board.

(c) The teacher assumes the roles of the two students and demonstrates what each is to do.

(d) The teacher calls for student volunteers to come up to the board, stand in front of the appropriate columns, and do the exercise.

(e) The teacher demonstrates folding the exercise page, and indicates which side each is to look at.

Step 2: Students form into pairs of students.

Step 3: Students fold their pages and do the exercise.

Step 4: The teacher can circulate from group to group assisting when asked or needed, encouraging students to listen carefully and to correct each other's sentences and pronunciation.

Step 5: When a pair has completed the exercise, the two students should change roles and do it again.

Complete

Completion activities provide writing practice and the use of individual cognitive skills. Students are asked, for example, to complete sentences, write questions, fill in forms, find and apply information from charts or maps, etc. Directions are specific for each activity. To explain and structure the activities, the teacher can use the chalkboard. As the students write individually or in small groups, the teacher circulates, giving assistance as needed or requested.

Concentration

The *Concentration* game is designed to practice new vocabulary and to teach discrimination between grammatical structures.

Step 1: The teacher cuts out the picture and word/sentence cards before class. The *Concentration* "deck" can be clipped together by a paper clip or kept in an envelope. The number of "decks" needed will be equal to the number of groups playing.

Step 2: Students sit in groups of three to five. The picture and word/sentence cards are shuffled and placed face down on a desk with the picture cards on one side, and the word/sentence cards on the other. The first player turns up a picture card and says the word or sentence that corresponds to the picture. The player then turns up a word/sentence card trying to match the picture. If the cards match, the student keeps them. If not, they are both replaced face down in the original position. The next student tries to match two cards in the same manner.

Step 3: The play continues until all the cards are matched. The teacher circulates from group to group assisting when asked. When the students finish the game, the teacher checks their cards, pointing out errors, but letting the students make the corrections themselves.

Step 4: An extension of this exercise is to give one student in the group all the word/sentence cards and distribute the picture cards to the other students in the group. The students take turns saying the word or utterance that describes their picture. If they say it correctly, the student with the word/sentence cards gives them the card that matches the picture.

Interaction

The Interaction Charts give the students a structured opportunity to practice their new language with one or two other students. Each activity begins with two or more questions about the topic.

Step 1: Students sit with a partner and ask each question. They mark their partner's response on the chart, usually by recording a "yes" or "no," circling an appropriate response or writing a single word. The students then switch roles. Often, other language and questions emerge as the students interact. The teacher should encourage the students to speak freely and gain confidence in their language use.

Step 2: Repeat Step 1 with a different partner. Most interaction charts ask the students to speak with two students.

Step 3: After the students have their partners' responses, several students should report their information back to the class. Typically, the teacher will ask a student, "Who(m) did you speak to?" and "What did he tell you?" The goal in this activity is correctly reporting information and using the new vocabulary. Do not focus on the correctness of the grammar.

Putting It Together

The last page in each unit gives the students the opportunity to practice and expand the coping and language skills emphasized in the unit in a freer mode of conversation. The activities on this page are based on an illustration of the coping skill in a particular situation.

Step 1: A lively illustration depicts the coping skills scene. As a whole class or in small groups, the students write down six to ten vocabulary words from the picture. If the students work in small groups, they then meet together as a whole class and share the lists which each group developed.

Step 2: The students talk about the picture. The teacher should take a low profile role in this activity. If prompting is necessary, he might say, "Talk about _____ (one of the characters in the scene)". A student will usually give just one or two sentences. The teacher should spend a minimum of ten minutes on this activity. Encourage the students to speak, even if the sentences they give are short or the same as those given by other students.

Step 3: Next, the students are asked to answer questions about the picture or to match short conversations about the picture.

When the exercise reads, "Discuss these questions," the students can ask and answer the questions in a small group or as a whole class. This is an oral exercise and the focus is both on correct information and on grammar. As a homework assignment, the students may write the answers to the questions.

When the exercise is matching, the students are asked to match short questions and answers which relate to the picture. As partners, the students memorize both parts of the interaction. Then, in small groups or as a whole class, the students divide into two groups. In Group A, the students look at the entire exercise. In Group B, the students cover the second column. A student from Group A gives the first part of the interaction from the first column. A student from Group B tries to answer or complete the interaction with the response from the second column. Continue until the students are comfortable with all the questions and answers. Then, switch groups.

Step 4: Role plays are the final activity. The students work together as partners and write a conversation about the picture or the coping skill area. The students have the support of the picture, the vocabulary and the questions or matching conversations. The teacher should circulate, giving assistance as needed and requested. The students practice the conversation without looking at their papers, and then stand in front of the class and act out their conversations. Remember that whenever this kind of freedom is given, a teacher may expect less perfection in students' language than he does during controlled practice.

Students may decide to tape record one or more of the conversations with the teacher's assistance. After the students complete the conversation, they can play back the tape one sentence at a time, repeating after the tape and writing the conversation on the chalkboard.

Gretchen Dowling
Barbara H. Foley
Howard Pomann

Acknowledgments

The development of this series has been the result of a long growth process. We wish to thank our many friends and colleagues who have given their support, shared their ideas, and increased our insights into the language-learning process and its application in the ESL classroom:

John Chapman, Ralph Colognori, Joyce Ann Custer, Mary Dolan, Jacqueline Flamm, Irene Frankel, Susan Lanzano, Elaine Langdon, Joann LaPerla, Darlene Larson, Marsha Malberg, Camille Mahon, Fred Malkemes, Joy Noren, Douglas Pillsbury, Deborah Pires, Sherri Preiss, Jennybelle Rardin, Sharon Seymour, Earl Stevick, and the faculty at the Institute for Intensive English, Union College.

Our thanks to Abraham Feria whose photos are used in Units 1, 2, 10, and 16. And special thanks goes to our spouses, Bill and June, for their patience and love.

Barbara Foley
Howard Pomann

1 Hello and Goodbye

Discuss

What's your name?
How are you?

Listen, Read and Say

Bill: Hello, I'm Bill.
Lisa: Hi. My name's Lisa.
Bill: Nice to meet you.
Lisa: Nice to meet you, too.

Practice this model.

> A: Hello. I'm _____.
> B: Hi, my name's _____.
> A: Nice to meet you.
> B: Nice to meet you, too.

complete

Complete these sentences.

1. Hello, I'm _____.
2. Hi, my name's _____.
3. Nice to meet _____.
4. Nice to _____ you, too.
5. My teacher's name is _____.

2

Bill: Hi, Lisa.
Lisa: Hi, Bill. How are you?
Bill: Great. And you?
Lisa: Fine, thanks.

Practice
Practice

Practice this model with the pictures below.

A:	How are you?
B:	____Great____, thank you.

A:	How's everything?
B:	____Great____, thanks.

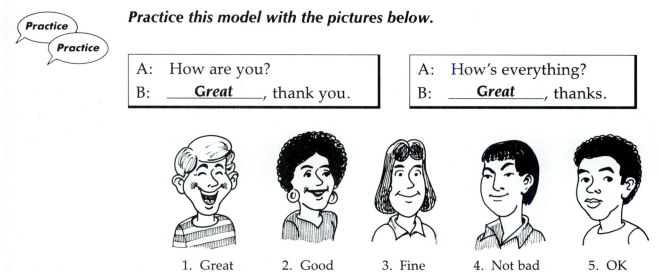

1. Great   2. Good   3. Fine   4. Not bad   5. OK

Interaction

Ask five students these questions. Write their answers in the chart below.

What's your name?
How are you?

STUDENT	HOW ARE YOU?
Maria	*Not bad.*

Listen, Read and Say

Bill: Goodbye, Lisa.
Lisa: Bye, Bill.
Bill: Have a good weekend.
Lisa: You too. See you on Monday.

Practice
Practice

Practice these expressions with the teacher.

Goodbye.
Bye.
Have a good weekend.
Have a nice weekend.
Have a good day.
Take it easy.
See you.
See you later.
See you tomorrow.
See you on Sunday.
See you on _____.

Sunday	Monday	Tuesday	Wednesday	Thursday	Friday	Saturday

Interaction

Match these short conversations. Practice them with a partner.

Hi.   Good, thanks.
How are you?   Hello.
Nice to meet you.   You have a nice weekend, too.
Have a nice weekend.   Nice to meet you, too.
See you on Monday.   Bye.
Goodbye.   See you.

HELLO AND GOODBYE

Talk about each picture. What are the people saying?

Hello   Goodbye

Write a response to these statements.

1. How are you?   _____ *Fine, thanks.* _____
2. Nice to meet you.   _____
3. Goodbye.   _____
4. See you on Saturday.   _____
5. How's everything?   _____
6. Hi!   _____
7. Have a good weekend.   _____

Role play

With another student, write and practice a conversation between two people saying "Hello" and two people saying "Good-bye." Present your dialogue to the class.

2 Introductions

Discuss

What's your name?
Where are you from?
Where are the students
   in your class from?

Listen, Read and Say

Ana: Hello, I'm Ana. I'm in your
          English class.
Julia: Hi, my name's Julia.
Ana: What country are you from?
Julia: I'm from Peru. And you?
Ana: I'm from Colombia.

Practice
   Practice

Practice this model. Tell the name of the country each person is from.

| _____ **He** _____ is from ____ **Colombia** ____ . |
| _____ **He'** _____s from ____ **Colombia** ____ . |

| They are from ____ **Japan** ____ . |
| They're from _____ **Japan** _____ . |

1. COLUMBIA   2. JAPAN   3. MEXICO   4. RUSSIA

5. POLAND   6. CUBA   7. SAUDI ARABIA   8. CHINA

Practice
   Practice

Practice this model with the teacher. Tell the name of your country.

| A: Where are you from? |
| B: I'm from _____ . |

Practice this model with the people and the countries below.

A: Where is ____*he*____ from?	A: Where are they from?
B: ___*He'*___s from ___**Haiti**___.	B: They're from ___*Puerto Rico*___.

1. HAITI

2. PUERTO RICO

3. ISRAEL

4. CAMBODIA

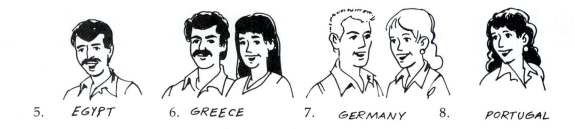

5. EGYPT   6. GREECE   7. GERMANY   8. PORTUGAL

Partner Exercise

Ask and answer questions about each person.

Student 1	**Student 2**
Where / he?	***Listen carefully and help Student 1.***
Where is he from?	

Student 1	Student 2
1. Where / he?	1. Where is he from?
2. He / Peru.	2. He's from Peru.
3. Where / she?	3. Where is she from?
4. She / Ecuador.	4. She's from Ecuador.
5. Where / they?	5. Where are they from?
6. They / Egypt.	6. They're from Egypt.
7. Where / he?	7. Where is he from?
8. He / Vietnam.	8. He's from Vietnam.
9. Where / they?	9. Where are they from?
10. They / Hungary.	10. They're from Hungary.
11. Where / you?	11. Where are you from?
12. I / _____.	12. I'm from _____.

(FOLD HERE)

7

 **CONCEN** **TRATION** *Cut out and play the Concentration Game on page 83. Match each picture with the correct sentence.*

 *complete*

Complete these questions and answers.

1. **Where** **are** they from?   **They're** **from** El Salvador.
2. _____ _____ he from?   _____ _____ Italy.
3. _____ _____ she from?   _____ _____ Puerto Rico.
4. _____ _____ he from?   _____ _____ Korea.
5. _____ _____ they from?   _____ _____ Israel.
6. _____ _____ she from?   _____ _____ Kenya.
7. _____ _____ he from?   _____ _____ Honduras.
8. _____ _____ they from?   _____ _____ Thailand.
9. _____ _____ she from?   _____ _____ Germany.
10. _____ _____ you from?   _____ _____ _____.

 Interaction

Ask five students these questions. Write their names and countries in the chart below.

What's your name?

My name's _____.

Where are you from?

I'm from _____.

NAME	COUNTRY
Maria	*Mexico*

THE WORLD MAP

Putting It Together

Talk about the people on this map. What countries are they from? Who is from each country?

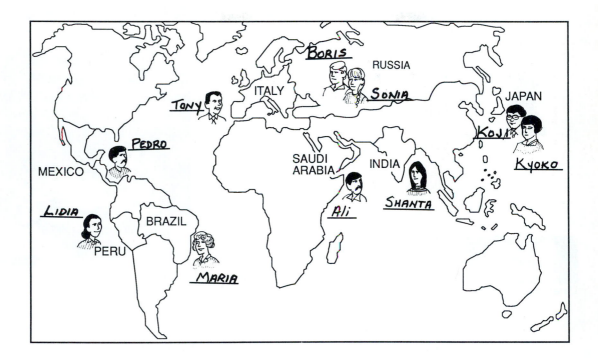

Match these short conversations about the map. Practice them with a partner.

Hello. My name is Koji.	He's from Mexico.
Where are you from?	They're from Russia.
What country is Pedro from?	Hi. I'm Shanta.
Where are Sonia and Boris from?	No, he's from Italy.
Is Tony from Peru?	I'm from Japan.

Role play

With another student, write and practice a conversation between two students. Introduce yourselves and talk about your countries. Present your dialogue to the class.

3 Your Name and Telephone Number

Discuss

What's your first name?
What's your last name?
What's your middle name?
Are you married?
What's your maiden name?

Listen, Read and Say

Mr. Hunt: What's your name?
Sonia: Sonia Romero.
Mr. Hunt: Spell your last name, please.
Sonia: R-O-M-E-R-O.
Mr. Hunt: And your first name?
Sonia: Sonia, S-O-N-I-A.
Mr. Hunt: What's your telephone number?
Sonia: 754-2341.
Mr. Hunt: Thank you.

Practice the letters with the teacher.

A B C D E F G H I J K L M N O P Q R S T U V W X Y Z

ABCDEFGHIJKLMNOPQRSTUVWXYZ

a b c d e f g h i j k l m n o p q r s t u v w x y z

abcdefghijklmnopqrstuvwxyz

Practice this conversation with the teacher.

Teacher:	What's your name?
You:	_____
Teacher:	Spell it, please.
You:	_____

The teacher will slowly spell the names of nine students in the class. Write each name. Then, read the name.

1. _____   4. _____   7. _____
2. _____   5. _____   8. _____
3. _____   6. _____   9. _____

Interaction

Talk to four students in your class. Ask four students their names and how to spell them. Write their names in the chart below.

What's your first name? Spell it, please.
What's your last name? Spell it, please.

STUDENT	FIRST NAME	LAST NAME
	Maria	*Campos*
1.		
2.		
3.		
4.		

complete

Complete these forms with your name.

PRINT YOUR FULL NAME _____

Mr.
Ms. _____
    LAST NAME   FIRST NAME   MIDDLE INITIAL

| | | | | | | | | | | | | | | | | | | |
LAST NAME   FIRST NAME   MIDDLE INITIAL

APPLICANT'S — LAST NAME   FIRST NAME   MIDDLE INITIAL

SIGNATURE _X_____

Practice
Practice

Practice saying these number with your teacher.

1	2	3	4	5	6	7	8	9	0
one	two	three	four	five	six	seven	eight	nine	oh/zero

Practice
Practice

Practice saying these telephone numbers using the model below.

A: What's your telephone number?
B: 362-5419. (three-six-two   five-four-one-nine)

1. 362-5419
2. 378-2316
3. 336-3111
4. 857-4269
5. 941-0927

6. (213) 853-7070
7. (212) 253-2481
8. (415) 455-1573
9. (713) 634-2800
10. Your telephone number.

**Partner
Exercise**

Practice these telephone numbers.

Student 1   **Student 2**
Say these telephone numbers.   *Listen carefully and help Student 1.*

1. 255-6219
2. 439-6140
3. 594-2209
4. 799-1628
5. 481-0683
6. (415) 874-4187
7. (212) 638-1249
8. (312) 238-1147
9. (512) 679-3122
10. (201) 533-1864

1. two-five-five six-two-one-nine
2. four-three-nine six-one-four-oh
3. five-nine-four two-two-oh-nine
4. seven-nine-nine one-six-two-eight
5. four-eight-one oh-six-eight-three
6. four-one-five eight-seven-four four-one-eight-seven
7. two-one-two six-three-eight one-two-four-nine
8. three-one-two two-three-eight one-one-four-seven
9. five-one-two six-seven-nine three-one-two-two
10. two-oh-one five-three-three one-eight-six-four

Listen as your teacher tells you these important telephone numbers. Then write them.

School: _____   Hospital: _____

Police: _____   Rescue Squad: _____

Fire Department: _____   Poison Control: _____

PERSONAL FORMS

Putting It Together

Complete these forms with your name, telephone number, and Social Security number.

Print your full name _____

Telephone Number (___) _____

NAME _____

SOCIAL SECURITY NUMBER _____

| | | | | | | | | | | | | | | | | | | | |
NAME   LAST   FIRST   MIDDLE INITIAL

| | | | — | | | — | | | |
TELEPHONE NUMBER

PLEASE PRINT — LAST NAME   FIRST NAME   MAIDEN NAME

SS # _____

NAME _____

PHONE (___) _____

4 Your Address and Birthdate

Discuss

Where do you live?
What's your address?
Do you live in a house
    or in an apartment?

Listen, Read and Say

Mr. Ferraro:	What's your address?
Ms. Burak:	62 Alamo Street, San Antonio.
Mr. Ferraro:	And the zip code?
Ms. Burak:	78205.
Mr. Ferraro:	What's your date of birth?
Ms. Burak:	5-24-64.

Practice
Practice

Practice saying these numbers and addresses with the teacher.

11	12	13	14	15	16	17	18	19
eleven	twelve	thirteen	fourteen	fifteen	sixteen	seventeen	eighteen	nineteen

10	20	30	40	50	60	70	80	90
ten	twenty	thirty	forty	fifty	sixty	seventy	eighty	ninety

6	six Main Street
16	sixteen Main Street
362	three sixty-two Main Street
36-25	thirty-six twenty-five Main Street
6524	sixty-five twenty-four Main Street

CONCEN | TRATION

Cut out and play the Concentration Game on page 85. Match each number with the correct word.

14

Practice these addresses.

Student 1	Student 2
Say the full address.	*Listen carefully and help Student 1.*

(FOLD HERE)

Student 1	Student 2
1. 32 Central Avenue	1. thirty-two Central Avenue
2. 756 Bay Street	2. seven fifty-six Bay Street
3. 5 York Avenue	3. five York Avenue
4. 16 Temple Place	4. sixteen Temple Place
5. 372 Summit Road	5. three seventy-two Summit Road
6. 84 Ocean Drive	6. eighty-four Ocean Drive
7. 159 Park Street	7. one fifty-nine Park Street
8. 33-11 First Place	8. thirty-three eleven First Place
9. 4592 Tenth Ave.	9. forty-five ninety-two Tenth Avenue
10. 1835 6th Avenue	10. eighteen thirty-five Sixth Avenue

Practice this model with the addresses below.

A: What's ____his____ address?
B: It's ____35 North Avenue____ .

A: What's ____their____ address?
B: It's ____356 Fourth Street____ .

1.   2.   3.

4.   5.   6.

7.   8.   9.

Look at the people. Complete these sentences with his, her, **or** their.

1. What's _____ **his** _____ address?

2. What's _____ address?

3. What's _____ address?

4. What's _____ address?

5. What's _____ address?

6. _____ address is 15 Bleeker Street.

7. _____ address is 237 Park Avenue, Apartment 4.

8. _____ address is 45 Kennedy Drive.

9. _____ address is 34-96 Broad Street.

10. _____ address is 53 South Street, Apartment 9B.

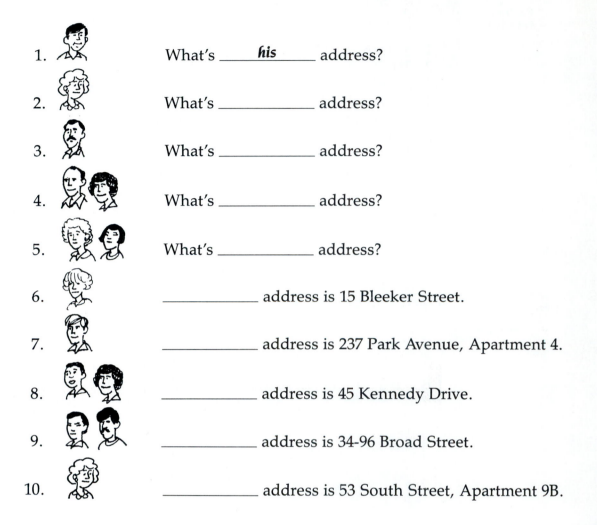

 **Practice this model with the teacher.**

A:	What's your date of birth?
	or
	What's your birthdate?
B:	__ **5** / **1 5** / **6 7** .

 **Write these birthdates.**

1. May 15, 1967   **5/15/67**   6. January 17, 1981 _____
2. September 14, 1947 _____   7. March 24, 1955   _____
3. April 21, 1971   _____ 8. February 9, 1962 _____
4. July 4, 1976   _____ 9. October 12, 1959 _____
5. November 11, 1973 _____   10. June 8, 1978   _____

PERSONAL FORMS

Complete these forms with your name, address, date of birth, telephone number, and Social Security number.

NAME _____

ADDRESS _____

CITY _____

STATE/ZIP _____

Mr.
Mrs.
Miss _____

Address _____

City _____

State _____ Zip _____

Name: _____
      FIRST   LAST

Maiden Name: _____

Address: _____
      STREET

_____
CITY   STATE   ZIP CODE

Telephone No: _____

Soc. Sec. No.: _____

☐ Mr. ☐ MS. _____

Address _____

City _____ State ____ Zip ____

LAST NAME

FIRST NAME

ADDRESS — STREET

CITY

ST.

ZIP CODE

DATE OF BIRTH ➤

MO. | DAY | YR.

Name and Home Address (Please Print)
Last

First

Middle Initial

Social Security Number

☐ Male
☐ Female

Date of Birth
Mo. | Day | Yr.

Number   Street   City   State   Zip Code

Marital Status
☐ Single ☐ Divorced
☐ Married ☐ Widowed

Role play

Ask two students these questions. Fill in the information on the forms below.

What's your name?
What's your address? What's your zip code?
What's your telephone number?
What's your Social Security number?
What's your date of birth?

APPLICANT'S — *LAST NAME*   *FIRST NAME*   MIDDLE INITIAL

APPLICANT'S RESIDENCE—   CITY   STATE

SOC. SEC. NO.

PRINT YOUR FULL NAME_____ Social Security No. _____

ADDRESS_____ CITY_____ STATE_____

5 Family

Do you have a big family?
How many brothers and sisters
   do you have?
How many children do you have?
Is your family here or
   in your native country?

Listen, Read and Say

Jill:	Here's a picture of my family.
Peter:	Who's the woman with the long hair?
Jill:	That's my sister.
Peter:	And the man with the mustache?
Jill:	That's my brother-in-law.

Practice

Practice

Practice this model. Talk about the relationships in the family tree below. Use the vocabulary to help you.

Helen is John's mother .	**Steven is Jenny's brother** .

mother	father	daughter	son
wife	husband	aunt	uncle
sister	brother	niece	nephew
grandmother	grandfather	sister-in-law	brother-in-law
granddaughter	grandson	mother-in-law	father-in-law

PAUL   HELEN

BOB   CAROL   JOHN   MARY

STEVEN   JENNY   KIM   KEN

Complete these sentences about the family picture.

1. _____ is John's daughter.
2. _____ is John's sister.
3. _____ is John's son.
4. _____ is John's nephew.
5. _____ is John's niece.
6. _____ is Jenny's brother.
7. _____ is Jenny's aunt.
8. _____ is Jenny's uncle.
9. _____ is Jenny's father.
10. _____ is Jenny's cousin.
11. _____ is Ken's mother.
12. _____ is Carol's husband.
13. _____ is John's daughter.
14. _____ is John's father.
15. _____ is Jenny's brother.
16. _____ is Mary's niece.
17. _____ is Bob's sister-in-law.
18. _____ is Ken's aunt.
19. _____ is Ken's grandfather.
20. _____ is Paul's son-in-law.

Practice this model with the people in the illustrations below.

A: Who's the _____ with the _____?
B: That's my _____.

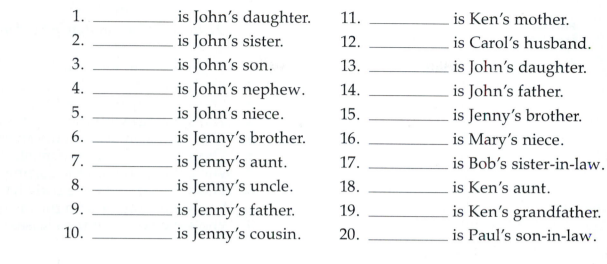

1. the sunglasses
   uncle

2. the short hair
   sister

3. the long hair
   aunt

4. the mustache
   father

5. the beard
   brother

6. the curly hair
   mother

7. the big hat
   cousin

8. the big earrings
   niece

9. the pipe
   grandfather

**Partner
Exercise**

Ask a *Who* question about each family member.

Student 1	**Student 2**
man / beard	*Listen carefully and help Student 1.*
Who's the man with the beard?	

1. man / beard
2. woman / sunglasses
3. boy / hat
4. girl / long necklace
5. woman / short hair
6. man / mustache
7. man / earring
8. girl / curly hair
9. woman / big earrings
10. boy / glasses

(FOLD HERE)

1. Who's the man with the beard?
2. Who's the woman with the sunglasses?
3. Who's the boy with the hat?
4. Who's the girl with the long necklace?
5. Who's the woman with the short hair?
6. Who's the man with the mustache?
7. Who's the man with the earring?
8. Who's the girl with the curly hair?
9. Who's the woman with the big earrings?
10. Who's the boy with the glasses?

Draw the faces. Then, write a question and answer.

1. Who's the ___woman___ with the ___big earrings___?
   That's my ___sister___.

2. Who's the _____ with the _____?
   That's my _____.

3. Who's the _____ with the _____?
   That's my _____.

4. Who's the _____ with the _____?
   That's my _____.

5. Who's the _____ with the _____?
   That's my _____.

A FAMILY

Putting
It
Together

Talk about this family picture. Write the new vocabulary on the picture.

ALEX   KATE   MARIE   BILL   STEVE   DONNA   LISA   DAN

Match these short conversations about the family picture. Practice them with a partner.

Is this a picture of your family?   That's my brother.

Who's the man with the beard?   She's 62 years old.

Is the woman with the hat your mother?   Yes, it is.

How old is your mother?   That's my sister-in-law.

Who's the woman with the long hair?   Thank you.

Your family is good looking.   Yes, she is.

Role play

Bring in pictures of your family. With another student, write and practice a conversation about the photos. Present your dialogue to the class.

6 School

Discuss

Are you married?
Do you have any children?
How old are they?
What grades are they in?

Listen, Read and Say

Sara: Are you married?
Doris: No, I'm single. How about you?
Sara: I'm married.
Doris: Do you have any children?
Sara: Yes, I have two boys.
Doris: How old are they?
Sara: Brian is fifteen. He's in tenth grade.
         Adam is eleven. He's in fifth grade.

Practice
Practice

Practice this model with the children shown in the pictures below.

A:	How old is she?
B:	*Tessa is nine years old* .

A:	How old are they?
B:	*Alex is six years old* .
	Sonia is four months old .

1. Tessa
   9

2. Andre
   14

3. Carmen
   13

4. Alex and Sonia
   6   4 months

5. Darold and Teresa
   8   11

6. Melissa, Jeffrey, and Steven
   15   5   3

THE SCHOOL SYSTEM IN THE UNITED STATES

SCHOOL	GRADES	
elementary	K–6	K–5
middle school		6–8
junior high school	7–9	
high school	10–12	9–12

Practice **Practice**

Practice saying these numbers with your teacher.

1st	**2nd**	**3rd**	**4th**	**5th**	**6th**
first	second	third	fourth	fifth	sixth

7th	**8th**	**9th**	**10th**	**11th**	**12th**
seventh	eighth	ninth	tenth	eleventh	twelfth

Partner Exercise

Say the grade and age for each child.

Student 1

Sarah   7   2nd
Sarah is seven years old.
She's in second grade.

1. Sarah   7   2nd
2. Melissa   15   10th
3. Kevin   8   3rd
4. Angela   11   5th
5. Mary   12   6th
6. Andre   14   9th
7. Luis   6   1st
8. Pierre   16   11th
9. Carmen   13   8th
10. Kim   5   kindergarten

(FOLD HERE)

Student 2
Listen carefully and help Student 1.

1. Sarah is seven years old.
   She's in second grade.
2. Melissa is 15 years old.
   She's in tenth grade.
3. Kevin is 8 years old.
   He's in third grade.
4. Angela is 11 years old.
   She's in fifth grade.
5. Mary is 12 years old.
   She's in sixth grade.
6. Andre is 14 years old.
   He's in ninth grade.
7. Luis is 6 years old.
   He's in first grade.
8. Pierre is 16 years old.
   He's in eleventh grade.
9. Carmen is 13 years old.
   She's in eighth grade.
10. Kim is 5 years old.
    She's in kindergarten.

complete

Answer these questions about the four students.

Anna	Pierre	Kevin	Kim
17	16	8	7
11th	10th	3rd	1st

1. Is Anna 17 years old? _____ **Yes, she is.** _____
2. Is she in junior high school? _____
3. Is she in 10th grade? _____
4. Is Pierre in high school? _____
5. Is he in 11th grade? _____
6. Is Kevin in middle school? _____
7. Is he eight years old? _____
8. Is Kim in elementary school? _____
9. Is Kim in first grade? _____
10. Is she seven years old? _____

Interaction

Ask three students these questions about their families. Fill in their answers in the chart below.

Are you married?
Do you have any children
    or brothers and sisters?
What are their names?
How old is _____?
What grade is _____ in?

STUDENT	MARITAL STATUS	NAMES	AGES	GRADES
Maria	M	*Julia* *Marc*	9 12	4th 7th

24

SCHOOL

Talk about these students. How old are they? What grades are they in? Where are they going to school? How are they going to school? Write the new vocabulary on the picture.

Match these short conversations about the students. Practice them with a partner.

Are you married?   Jack and Kathy.

Do you have any children?   She's sixteen.

What are their names?   Yes, I am.

How old is Kathy?   Yes, I have a boy and a girl.

What grade is Kathy in?   No, he's in first grade.

Is Jack in kindergarten?   She's in tenth grade.

Role play

With another student, write and practice a conversation about your families. Ask about names, ages, and grades. Present your dialogue to the class.

25

7 Transportation

Where is the train or bus station
    in your town or city?
Do you sometimes travel by bus or train?
    Where?
How much is a ticket?

Listen, Read and Say

Larry: A one-way ticket to Stamford, please.
Agent: That's $38.50.
Larry: When's the next train?
Agent: At 10:30.
Larry: Thank you.

Practice
  Practice

Practice these amounts with the teacher. There are two ways to say some amounts.

$ 5.00   five dollars

$ 9.25   nine twenty-five
                nine dollars and twenty-five cents

$ 32.75   thirty-two seventy-five
                thirty-two dollars and seventy-five cents

$125.50   one twenty-five fifty
                one hundred and twenty-five dollars and fifty cents

Practice
  Practice

Practice these models with the tickets below.

| A: A one-way ticket to **Boston**. |
| B: That's $ _____ **18.25** _____ . |

| A: A round-trip ticket to **Boston**. |
| B: That's $ _____ **32.50** _____ . |

1. *Boston*
one-way $18.25
round-trip $32.50

2. *Philadelphia*
one-way $12.50
round-trip $19.75

3. *San Francisco*
one-way $34.75
round-trip $57.25

5. *Miami*
one-way $65.00
round-trip $105.00

6. *Houston*
one-way $24.50
round-trip $37.25

7. *Santa Fe*
one-way $57.00
round-trip $81.50

Cut out and play the Concentration Game on page 85. Match the figure and the dollar amounts.

Write the amount in words.

1. $ 8.25   _____*eight dollars and twenty-five cents*_____
2. $ 6.00   _____
3. $ 14.50   _____
4. $ 19.75   _____
5. $ 23.20   _____
6. $ 35.40   _____
7. $ 87.60   _____
8. $196.15   _____
9. $239.35   _____
10. $500.00   _____

Practice this model with the clocks below.

Practice
Practice

A:	When's the next train?
B:	It's at ____**2:00**____.

When is the next train?

Student 1

Give the time of the next train.

Student 2
Listen carefully and help Student 1.

(FOLD HERE)

1. 1. The next train is at two twenty-five.

2. 2. The next train is at five o'clock.

3. 3. The next train is at seven-thirty.

4. 4. The next train is at three-fifteen.

5. 5. The next train is at eight forty-five.

6. 6. The next train is at two thirty-eight.

7. 7. The next train is at twelve-thirty.

8. 8. The next train is at four-o-seven.

9. 9. The next train is at one-fifteen.

10. 10. The next train is at eight forty-five.

28

THE TRAIN STATION

Talk about each of these trains. When is the train leaving? What track is it on? Is it on time? What are these people doing?

Match these short conversations. Practice them with a partner.

I'd like a one-way ticket to Boston.	No. It's on track 8.
Is this the train to Philadelphia?	It's on track 3.
What track is the train to Miami on?	No, it's on time.
When is the train to Washington?	That's $18.50.
Is the train to Newark late?	No, it's an hour late.
Is the train to Trenton on time?	At 3:15.

Role play

With another student, write and practice a conversation between a ticket agent and a passenger. Buy a ticket and ask for information. Present your dialogue to the class.

8 Downtown

Discuss

Where do you live?
What public buildings are there in your community?
Where is the library? the post office? the police station?

Listen, Read and Say

Ann: Where's the library?
Tom: It's on Front Street next to the park.

Practice Practice

Practice this model with the buildings and streets below.

> A: Excuse me. Where's the <u>*train station*</u> ?
> B: It's on <u>**Front Street**</u> .
> A: Thank you.

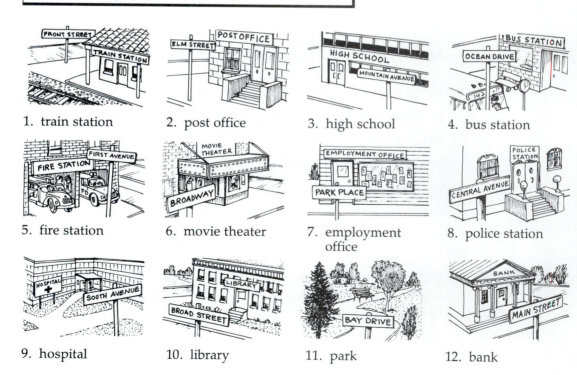

1. train station
2. post office
3. high school
4. bus station
5. fire station
6. movie theater
7. employment office
8. police station
9. hospital
10. library
11. park
12. bank

Practice this model with the buildings below.

| Where is the police station? It's *next to* the hospital. | Where is the hospital? It's *across from* the employment office. | Where's the fire station? It's *between* the bank and the park. |

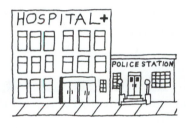

1. hospital   2. library   3. elementary school

4. post office   5. train station   6. fire station

7. movie theater   8. employment office   9. police station

CONCEN **TRATION** *Cut out and play the Concentration Game on page 87. Match the building and the location.*

Partner Exercise

Look at the picture and give the location of each building.

Student 1	Student 2
Give the location of each building	*Listen carefully and help Student 1.*

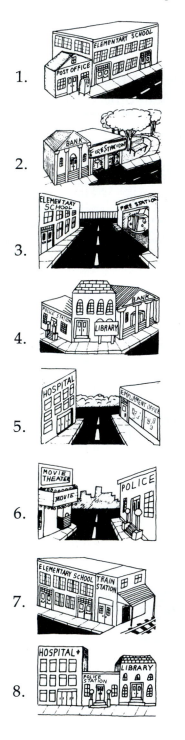

1.

2.

3.

4.

5.

6.

7.

8.

(FOLD HERE)

1. The post office is next to the elementary school.

2. The fire station is between the bank and the park.

3. The elementary school is across from the fire station.

4. The library is between the police station and the bank.

5. The employment office is across from the hospital.

6. The movie theater is across from the police station.

7. The train station is next to the elementary school.

8. The police station is between the hospital and the library.

A STREET MAP

Talk about the buildings and places on this street map. Tell their locations.

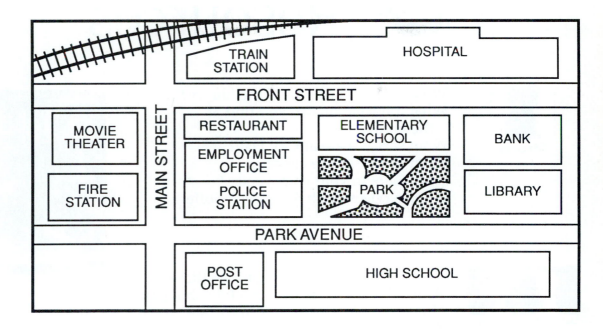

Discuss these questions.

1. Where is the hospital?
2. Is the train station next to the hospital?
3. Is the bank on Front Street?
4. Where is the elementary school?
5. Where is the movie theater?
6. Is the fire station on Front Street?
7. Where is the employment office?
8. Is the high school across the street from the hospital?
9. Where is the police station?
10. Where is the post office?

Role play

Talk with a partner from your community. Write the location of these places.

1. The library _____.
2. The post office _____.
3. The high school _____.
4. The police station _____.
5. The fire station _____.
6. The train station _____.
7. The bus station _____.
8. The park _____.

33

9 Community Resources

Discuss

What can you take out of the library?
What information can you find at
   the library?
What services are at City Hall?
What social service agencies
   are there in your community?
What services do these agencies offer?

Listen, Read and Say

Jim: Hi. This is Jim. Is Shirley there?
Ann: No, Jim. She'll be back in about an hour.
Jim: What's she doing? She's late.
Ann: She's at the library. She's writing a report.
Jim: Please ask her to call me.
Ann: OK.

Practice *Practice*

Practice this model with these places and activities.

A:	What is he doing?
B:	He's _looking for a book_.

A:	What is she doing?
B:	She's _returning some books_.

1. look for a book

2. return some books

3. take out some books

4. pay taxes

5. register to vote

6. get a dog license

34

A: What are you doing?
B: I'm **depositing some money**.

A: What are they doing?
B: They're **cashing a check**.

1. deposit some money

2. cash a check

3. take out some money

4. buy some stamps

5. mail some letters

6. send packages

Partner Exercise

What is each person doing?

Student 1

He / mail a letter
He is mailing a letter.

1. He / mail a letter
2. She / put money in her account.
3. She / take out a loan
4. They / talk with the principal

5. We / return some books
6. I / take out some books
7. They / register to vote
8. He / report an accident
9. She / pay a ticket
10. I / apply for unemployment

(FOLD HERE)

Student 2
Listen carefully and help Student 1.

1. He's mailing a letter.
2. She's putting money in her account.
3. She's taking out a loan.
4. They're talking with the principal.
5. We're returning some books.
6. I'm taking out some books.
7. They are registering to vote.
8. He's reporting an accident.
9. She's paying a ticket.
10. I'm applying for unemployment.

35

Cut out and play the Concentration Game on page 89. Match each action with the correct sentence.

 *complete*

Complete these questions and answers about the pictures.

1. What is he doing?

   He's taking out some books.

2. What is she doing?

   _____

3. What are they doing?

   _____

4. What is he doing?

   _____

5. What _____ you doing?

   _____

6. What _____ she doing?

   _____

7. What _____ they _____?

   _____

8. What _____ he _____?

   _____

9. What _____ she _____?

   _____

10. What _____ you _____?

    _____

THE LIBRARY

Putting It Together

Talk about this library. Where is each person? What is each person doing? Write the new vocabulary on the picture.

Role play

With another student, complete these sentences about agencies and services in your area.

1. At the post office, you can _____.
2. At the library, you can _____.
3. At the bank, you can _____.
4. At City Hall, you can _____.
5. At the police station, you can _____.
6. At the employment office, you can _____.
7. At the Motor Vehicle Agency, you can _____.

10 Supermarket

Discuss

What's the best supermarket
   in your area?
Why is it the best? Is it large?
Is the food fresh?
Are the prices good?
How often do you go
   to the supermarket?

Listen, Read and Say

Susan: Excuse me. Where's the salt?
Clerk: It's in aisle 3, in the back.
Susan: Thanks.

Practice **Practice**

Practice this model with the food items below:

A:	Excuse me. Where's the ____*milk*____?
B:	It's in aisle ____3____, in the back.

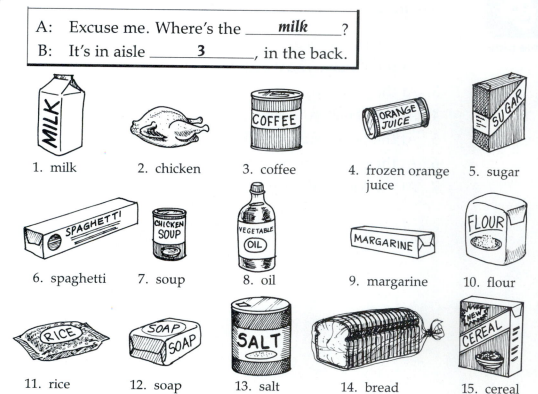

1. milk   2. chicken   3. coffee   4. frozen orange juice   5. sugar

6. spaghetti   7. soup   8. oil   9. margarine   10. flour

11. rice   12. soap   13. salt   14. bread   15. cereal

Practice this model with the food items below.

A: Excuse me. Where are the _____apples_____?
B: They're in aisle _____6_____, in the front.

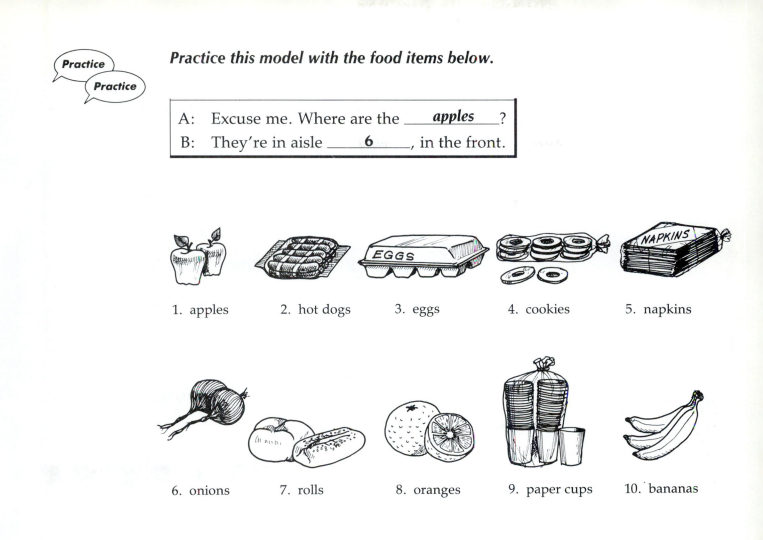

1. apples   2. hot dogs   3. eggs   4. cookies   5. napkins

6. onions   7. rolls   8. oranges   9. paper cups   10. bananas

Complete these questions and answers.

1. Where __is__ the coffee?   ____It's____ __in__ aisle 2.
2. Where _____ the apples?   _____ _____ aisle 4.
3. Where _____ the onions?   _____ _____ aisle 1.
4. Where _____ the salt?   _____ _____ aisle 5.
5. Where _____ the oil?   _____ _____ aisle 7.
6. Where _____ the sugar?   _____ _____ aisle 2.
7. Where _____ the napkins?   _____ _____ aisle 3.
8. Where _____ the bread?   _____ _____ aisle 6.
9. Where _____ the oranges?   _____ _____ aisle 6.
10. Where _____ the flour?   _____ _____ aisle 2.

CONCEN **TRATION** **Cut out and play the Concentration Game on page 91. Match each food picture with the correct question.**

39

Ask the location of each food item below.

Student 1		Student 2

Where is the coffee?

Student 2
Listen carefully and help Student 1.

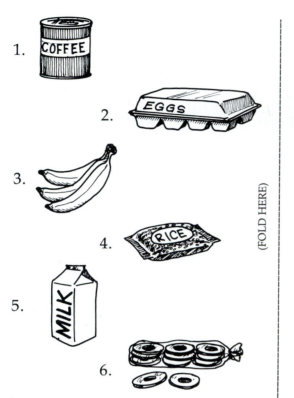

1.   COFFEE

2.   EGGS

3.

4.   RICE

5.   MILK

6.

(FOLD HERE)

1. Where's the coffee?

2. Where are the eggs?

3. Where are the bananas?

4. Where's the rice?

5. Where's the milk?

6. Where are the cookies?

Interaction

Ask three students these questions about the supermarket. Fill in their answers in the chart below.

What supermarket do you like?
Where is it?
How are the prices?
How's the quality of the food?

STUDENT	SUPERMARKET AND LOCATION	PRICES	QUALITY
		expensive not expensive	excellent good so-so
		expensive not expensive	excellent good so-so
		expensive not expensive	excellent good so-so

THE SUPERMARKET

Talk about this supermarket. Where is each person? What are they doing? Write the new vocabulary words on the picture.

Discuss these questions.

1. Where is Mrs. Wilson?
2. What is she buying?
3. What is she holding?
4. Who is Wanda?
5. What is she ringing up?
6. Is that the right price?
7. What is the clerk doing?
8. Where is Howard?
9. What's he carrying?
10. What is Terry asking Howard?
11. What is Howard answering?
12. What is Lisa putting in the cart?

Role play

With another student, write and practice a conversation between two people in a supermarket. Ask about the location of some items. Present your dialogue to the class.

11 Restaurants

Discuss

Do you have time to eat
    breakfast?
What do you eat for breakfast?
Do you have coffee or tea
    in the morning?
Do you sometimes eat
    out for breakfast?
Where?

Listen, Read and Say

Waitress: Are you ready to order?
Kathy: Yes. I'd like coffee and two eggs.
Waitress: How do you want your eggs?
Kathy: Scrambled.
Waitress: Anything else?
Kathy: A small orange juice, please.

Practice Practice

Practice this model with the food items below:

I'd like _____*coffee*_____.

or

I want _____*coffee*_____.

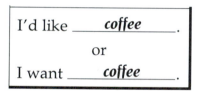

1. coffee   2. tea   3. cereal   4. two eggs   5. a small milk
   a cup of coffee   a cup of tea

6. a large orange   7. toast   8. an English   9. pancakes   10. a roll
   juice   muffin

42

Practice **Practice**

Practice this model with the menu items below.

> A: How do you want your eggs?
> B: ___**Scrambled**___, please.

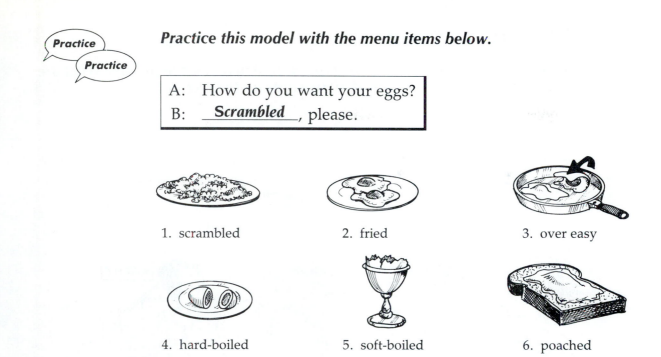

1. scrambled   2. fried   3. over easy

4. hard-boiled   5. soft-boiled   6. poached

Partner Exercise

Ask and answer questions about these orders.

Student 1	Student 2
How?	**Listen carefully and help Student 1.**
How do you want your eggs?	

Student 1

1. How?

2.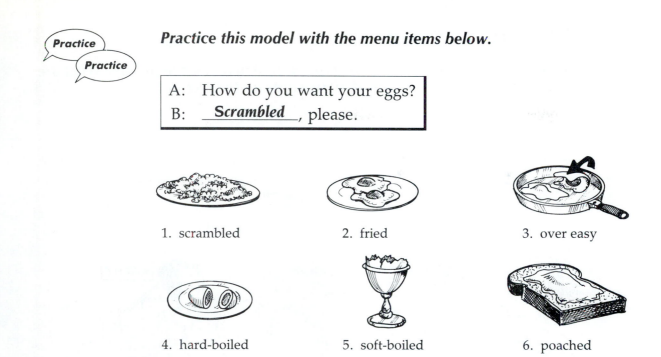

3. How?

4.

5. How?

6.

7. How?

8.

9. How?

10.

(FOLD HERE)

Student 2
Listen carefully and help Student 1.

1. How do you want your eggs?

2. Fried, please.

3. How do you want your eggs?

4. Hard-boiled, please.

5. How do you want your eggs?

6. Scrambled, please.

7. How do you want your eggs?

8. Poached, please.

8. How do you want your eggs?

10. Over easy, please.

43

THE COFFEE SHOP

Putting
It
Together

Talk about this coffee shop. What time is it? Where are the people? What are they doing? Write the new vocabulary words on the picture.

Match these short conversations in the coffee shop. Practice them with a partner.

Are you ready to order?	Yes, decaf please.
How do you want your eggs?	Apple juice.
Would you like some coffee?	Yes, I'd like two eggs.
What kind of juice do you want?	No, thanks. That's all.
Anything else?	Over easy.

44

BREAKFAST MENU

Role play

Look at the menu. With another student, practice a conversation between a customer and a waitress. The customer will order breakfast. The waitress will write down the order. Present your dialogue to the class.

Good Morning!

Special #1
Choice of Juice
TWO FRESH EGGS
Any Style
Home Fries
Toast and Butter
Coffee or Tea
$3.25

Special #2
Choice of Juice
GOLDEN BROWN
PANCAKES (3)
Butter and Maple Syrup
Coffee or Tea
$3.75

Special #3
Choice of Juice
FRENCH TOAST
Butter and Maple Syrup
Coffee or Tea
$3.75

Eggs
ONE EGG, Any Style	1.95
TWO EGGS, Any Style	2.15
PLAIN OMELETTE	3.15
CHEESE OMELETTE	3.95
ONION OMELETTE	3.55
HAM AND CHEESE OMELETTE	4.35
TWO EGGS on Roll	1.90

From the Griddle
3 GOLDEN BROWN PANCAKES	2.75
BLUEBERRY PANCAKES	3.95
APPLE PANCAKES	3.95
FRENCH TOAST	2.75

Cereals
HOT CEREAL with Milk	1.50
COLD CEREAL with Milk	1.50

From the Bakery
CORN OR BLUEBERRY MUFFIN	.95
ENGLISH MUFFIN with Butter	.95
BAGEL with Cream Cheese	1.70
PASTRIES	1.25
TOAST with Butter and Jelly	.85

Side Orders
HOME FRIES	.85
FRENCH FRIES	.85
BACON, HAM or SAUSAGE	1.50

Beverages
JUICE	1.20
COFFEE or TEA	.65
HOT CHOCOLATE	.90
MILK	.80
CHOCOLATE MILK	.90

FOOD CHECK

ITEM	AMOUNT
TOTAL	

12 Clothes

Discuss

How's the weather in your area?
Which season do you like best?
  Why?
What do you wear in the winter?
  in the spring? in the summer?
  in the fall?

Listen, Read and Say

Salesperson: Can I help you?
Alex: Yes, I'm looking
  for a shirt.
Salesperson: What size are you?
Alex: Medium.
Salesperson: The shirts are here.
Alex: Thank you.

Practice
Practice

Practice this model with the clothes below.

A: Can I help you?
B: Yes, I'm looking for a ___*blouse*___.

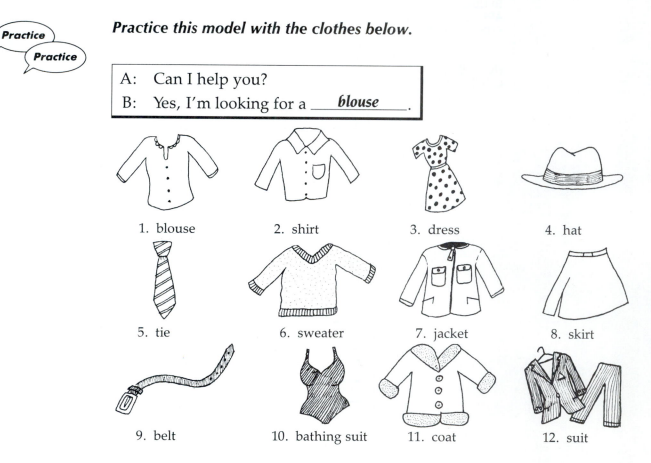

1. blouse   2. shirt   3. dress   4. hat

5. tie   6. sweater   7. jacket   8. skirt

9. belt   10. bathing suit   11. coat   12. suit

46

Practice this model with the clothes below.

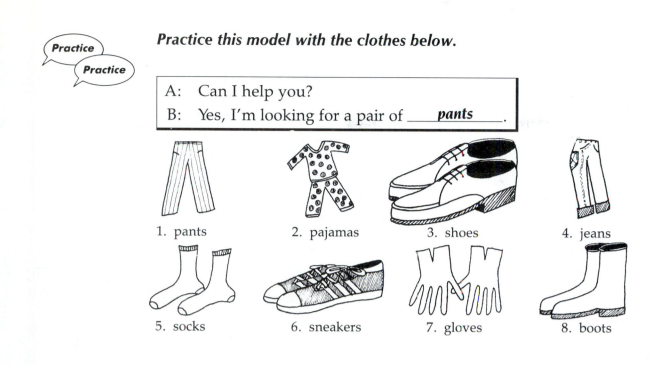

A:	Can I help you?
B:	Yes, I'm looking for a pair of _____ *pants* _____.

1. pants   2. pajamas   3. shoes   4. jeans

5. socks   6. sneakers   7. gloves   8. boots

CONCEN TRATION **Cut out and play the Concentration Game on page 91. Match each clothes picture with the correct sentence.**

Ask for each item in the clothes store.

Partner
Exercise

<table>
<tr><td align="center">**Student 1**
I'm looking for a hat.</td><td align="center">**Student 2**
Listen carefully and help Student 1.</td></tr>
</table>

1.	1. I'm looking for a hat.
2.	2. I'm looking for a skirt.
3.	3. I'm looking for a pair of pants.
4.	4. I'm looking for a jacket.
5.	5. I'm looking for a pair of gloves.
6.	6. I'm looking for a bathing suit.
7.	7. I'm looking for a dress.
8.	8. I'm looking for a pair of shoes.
9.	9. I'm looking for a pair of boots.
10.	10. I'm looking for a suit.

(FOLD HERE)

Complete one of these charts with your size.

MEN

Sweater S M L XL	Shirt S M L XL	Dress Shirt neck _____ sleeve _____

Men's Pants
  waist   _____
  length   _____
	Suit
	34 36 38 40 _____
	S R L
		Shoes
		  size _____

WOMEN

Sweater S M L XL	Top S M L XL	Blouse, Suit, Dress 4 6 8 10 12 14 16 18 junior: 5 7 9 11 13
Bra 30 32 34 36 38 A B C D	Pants, Slacks 6 8 10 12 14 16 18 junior: 5 7 9 11 13	Shoes size _____

Interaction

Work with a partner. In the boxes, write the clothes you wear in each kind of weather.

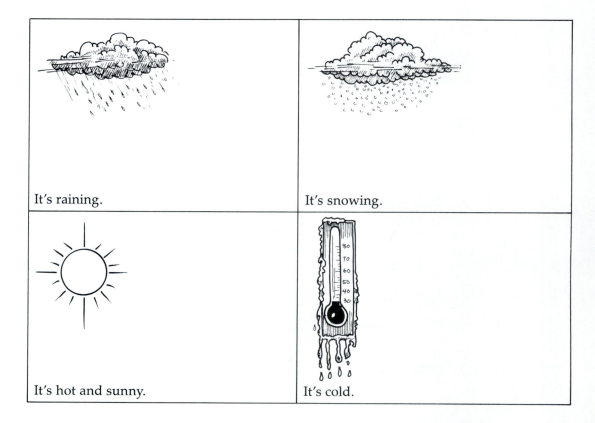

It's raining.

It's snowing.

It's hot and sunny.

It's cold.

THE CLOTHES STORE

Putting
It
Together

Talk about the people in this clothes store. Where are they? What are they doing? Write the new vocabulary words on the picture.

Match these short conversations in the clothes store. Practice them with a partner.

Can I help you? —————————————— Cash.

Excuse me. Where are the ties? —————— No, thanks. I'm just looking.

Can I return this?   Small.

What size are you?   They're over here.

Is that cash or charge?   Yes. Keep your receipt.

With another student, write and practice a conversation between a clerk and a customer in a clothes store. Ask the clerk for assistance. Present your dialogue to the class.

Role play

49

13 Prices

Discuss

Where do you go shopping for clothes?
What's a good store in this area
  for men's clothes?
  women's clothes?
  children's clothes?
When do stores have
  the best sales?

Listen, Read and Say

Joan: I like this suit.
How much is it?
Clerk: It's $79.99.
Joan: Thank you.

Practice
Practice

Practice this model with the clothes below.

| I like this ___**T-shirt**___ . | I like these ___*shorts*___ . |

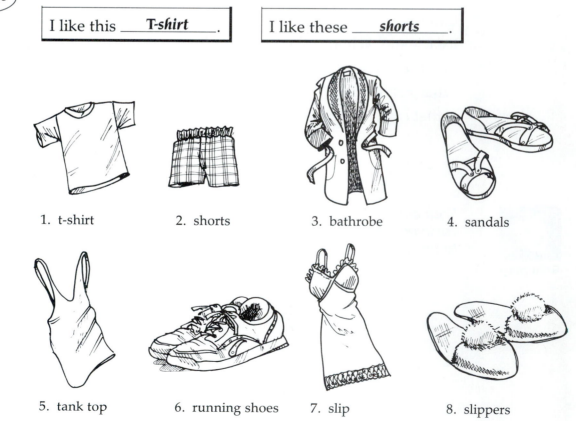

1. t-shirt   2. shorts   3. bathrobe   4. sandals

5. tank top   6. running shoes   7. slip   8. slippers

Practice this model with the clothes below.

A: I like this ___scarf___. How much is it? B: It's $___27___.	A: I like these ___earrings___. How much are they? B: They're $___55___.

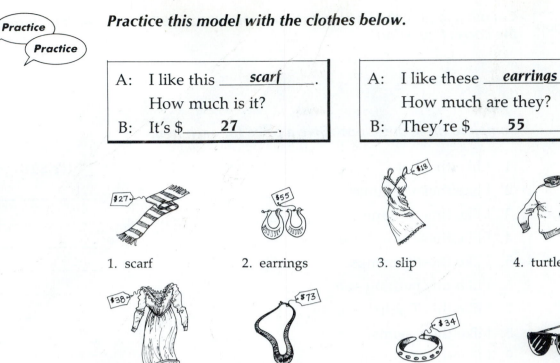

1. scarf   2. earrings   3. slip   4. turtleneck

5. nightgown   6. necklace   7. bracelet   8. sunglasses

Partner Exercise

Ask the price for each item in the clothes store.

Student 1
I like this necklace.
How much is it?

1.
2.
3.
4.
5.
6.
7.
8.
9.
10.

(FOLD HERE)

Student 2
Listen carefully and help Student 1.

1. I like this necklace.
   How much is it?

2. I like these earrings.
   How much are they?

3. I like this hat.
   How much is it?

4. I like these slippers.
   How much are they?

5. I like this bathrobe.
   How much is it?

6. I like these running shoes.
   How much are they?

7. I like these sunglasses.
   How much are they?

8. I like this scarf.
   How much is it?

9. I like this slip.
   How much is it?

10. I like these pants.
    How much are they?

Cut out and play the Concentration Game on page 93. Match each picture with the correct question.

Complete these questions. Give a price for each item.

1. I like this hat.   __How much is it__ ?   __It's $28.__ .
2. I like these pajamas.   _____ ?   _____ .
3. I like this turtleneck.   _____ ?   _____ .
4. I like these sunglasses.   _____ ?   _____ .
5. I like these earrings.   _____ ?   _____ .
6. I like this bathing suit.   _____ ?   _____ .
7. I like this T-shirt.   _____ ?   _____ .
8. I like these jeans.   _____ ?   _____ .
9. I like this nightgown.   _____ ?   _____ .
10. I like these stockings.   _____ ?   _____ .

Interaction

Ask two students these questions about a clothing store. Fill in their answers in the chart below.

What clothes store do you like?
Where is it?
How are the prices?
How's the quality?

STUDENT	STORE AND LOCATION	PRICES	QUALITY
Maria	Shoppers World on Front Street	expensive not expensive	excellent good so-so
		expensive not expensive	excellent good so-so
		expensive not expensive	excellent good so-so

AN AD FOR A SALE

Talk about the clothes ad and the prices. Write the new vocabulary on the picture.

CLOTHING MART WASHINGTON'S BIRTHDAY SALE
Feb. 17—24 • 10 a.m.-9 p.m.

40% Off
All gold and silver jewelry
Reg. $25 - $200
Now $15 - $120

25% Off
Solid and print sweaters
Men's S M L XL
Reg. $40-$80 **Now $30-$60**

20-33% Off
Women's and Junior Blouses
Orig. $32 - $48
Now $24-$36

2 for $20
Misses Turtlenecks
Reg. $20 each
S M L XL

$10-$20 Off
Entire stock of
Shoes and Boots
All Sizes

½ Price
Boys and Girls Jeans
Orig. $38-$72 **Now $19-$36**

Girls 4-14
Boys 4-18
Toddler 2-4T

Discuss these questions.

1. What store is this ad for?
2. When is the sale?
3. Why is the store having a sale?
4. What's on sale?
5. What's the discount for each item on sale?
6. What's the regular price for each item on sale?
7. What's the sale price for each item on sale?
8. What children's clothes are on sale?
9. What men's clothes are on sale?
10. Is this a good sale?

Role play

Bring in ads for clothing sales from a store in your area. With another student, write a few sentences about the sale prices, location and time. Present the information about the sale to the class.

 14 Health

Discuss

Who's your doctor?
When do you go to the doctor?
Do you speak English
  at the doctor's office?
What hospital do you go to
  in an emergency?

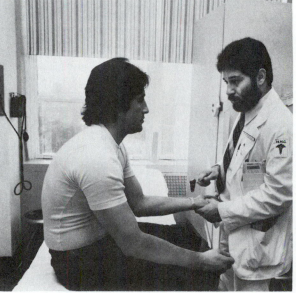

Listen, Read and Say

Andre: I don't feel well.
Doctor: What's the problem?
Andre: I have a cough.

Practice
  Practice

Practice this model with the problems below.

A: What's the problem?
B: I have __*a headache*__.

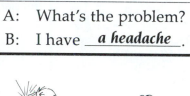

1. a headache   2. a stomachache   3. a toothache   4. a backache   5. an earache

Practice this model with the problems below.

A: What's the matter?
B: He has __*a cough*__.

A: What's the matter?
B: He has __*a fever*__.

1. a cough   2. a fever   3. a cold   4. a rash   5. a sore throat

54

CONCEN TRATION **Cut out and play the Concentration Game on page 95. Match the picture and the health problem.**

Partner Exercise

Describe the health problem.

Student 1
I / a cough
I have a cough.

1. I / a cough
2. I / a backache
3. He / a stomachache
4. She / a fever
5. He / a cold
6. I / a rash
7. She / an earache
8. I / a headache
9. He / a toothache
10. I / a sore throat

(FOLD HERE)

Student 2
Listen carefully and help Student 1.

1. I have a cough.
2. I have a backache.
3. He has a stomachache.
4. She has a fever.
5. He has a cold.
6. I have a rash.
7. She has an earache.
8. I have a headache.
9. He has a toothache.
10. I have a sore throat.

complete

Complete with have or has and a or an.

1. I ____have____ __a__ cough.
2. He _____ ____ headache.
3. She _____ ____ stomachache.
4. I _____ ____ cold.
5. I _____ ____ earache.
6. He _____ ____ toothache.
7. She _____ ____ sore throat.
8. I _____ ____ rash.
9. I _____ ____ backache.
10. She _____ ____ fever.

55

Interaction

Practice the names of the parts of the body with the teacher. Then, sit with another student and label the parts of the body. Use the vocabulary list below to help you.

head	neck	finger	toe
eyes	arm	chest	side
ear	shoulder	leg	back
mouth	elbow	knee	
nose	wrist	ankle	
tooth (teeth)	hand	foot (feet)	

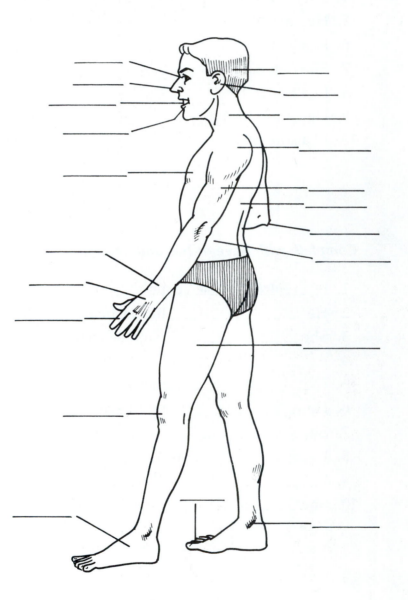

THE DOCTOR'S OFFICE

Talk about this doctor's office. Where is the doctor? Where is the nurse? What are they doing? What is the problem with each patient? What is each patient doing? Write the new vocabulary words on the picture.

MIKE

MEDICAL HISTORY FORM

MARGARET

SALLY   MRS. JONES

Match these short conversations between a doctor and a patient. Practice them with a partner.

What's the problem?

Are you getting enough sleep?

Does this hurt?

You should get lots of rest.

Take this prescription four times a day.

Drink a lot of liquids.

Yes, a little.

I have a sore throat and a cold.

Yes, about six hours a night.

I'll stay home from work tomorrow.

I'll drink a lot of juice.

Okay, that's every six hours.

Role play

With another student, write and practice a conversation between a patient and a doctor. The patient will talk about his health problems. The doctor will ask questions and give advice. Present your dialogue to the class.

15 The Drugstore

Discuss

What drugstore do you go to?
What over-the-counter medicines
   do you have at home?
In your country, do you need
   a prescription for medicine?
Are you allergic to anything?

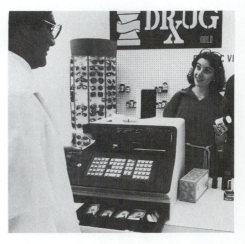

Listen, Read and Say

Pharmacist: Can I help you?
        Lee: I have an upset stomach.
             What do you recommend?
Pharmacist: Why don't you try this?
        Lee: How often should I take it?
Pharmacist: Four times a day.
        Lee: Thank you.

Practice *Practice*

Practice this model with the problems below.

My son has ___*a runny nose*___.   My children have ___*allergies*___.

1. my son
   a runny nose

2. my children
   allergies

3. I
   heartburn

4. my son
   diarrhea

5. my daughter
   an ear infection

6. my wife
   an upset stomach

7. I
   hay fever

8. my husband
   dandruff

58

9. my daughter
   a sunburn

10. my daughter
    a stiff neck

11. my children
    poison ivy

12. I
    a burn

Describe the health problem.

Student 1
I / a stiff neck
I have a stiff neck.

1. I / a stiff neck
2. My son / an ear infection
3. My daughter / a burn
4. I / a headache
5. My husband / a stomachache
6. I / heartburn
7. My son / a rash
8. My children / poison ivy
9. My wife / a backache
10. My child / hay fever

(FOLD HERE)

Student 2
Listen carefully and help Student 1.

1. I have a stiff neck.
2. My son has an ear infection.
3. My daughter has a burn.
4. I have a headache.
5. My husband has a stomachache.
6. I have heartburn.
7. My son has a rash.
8. My children have poison ivy.
9. My wife has a backache.
10. My child has hay fever.

Partner
Exercise

Complete with **have** or **has**.

1. My daughter _____**has**_____ a burn.

2. I _____ a sore throat.

3. My son _____ a runny nose.

4. My child _____ a cough.

5. My husband _____ dandruff.

6. My children _____ colds.

7. My son _____ diarrhea.

8. I _____ an upset stomach.

9. My daughter _____ a stiff neck.

10. My wife _____ a sunburn.

Interaction

Talk to another student. Describe each health problem. Your partner will suggest a product to try. Fill in the names of the products in the chart below.

Student 1:   What should I take for _____?
Student 2:   Why don't you try _____?

PROBLEM	PRODUCT
1. a headache	
2. a stomachache	
3. a fever	
4. a runny nose	
5. a burn	
6. diarrhea	
7. a cold	
8. a cough	
9. a sore throat	
10. a sunburn	

Read these labels. Then read the true–false statements below for each label. Circle T for true or F for false.

1.
Take one teaspoonful every 6 hours.

2.
Take one tablet before each meal.

3.
Chew one tablet twice a day.

4.
Put drops in eyes every 6 hours.

5.
Apply to rash four times a day.

6.
Take one pill three times a day with food.

1. You should take this medicine six times a day.   T   F
2. You should take this medicine after you eat.   T   F
3. You should take two tablets with every meal.   T   F
4. You should put drops in your eyes four times a day.   T   F
5. You should use this medicine for four days.   T   F
6. You should take this medicine with your meals.   T   F

THE DRUGSTORE

Talk about this drugstore. Who are the people? Where are they? What are they doing? Write the new vocabulary words on the picture.

Match these short conversations between a customer and a pharmacist. Practice them with a partner.

Please fill this prescription.

How often should I take this?

Do I take this before or after meals?

I'd like to renew a prescription.

I have a bad headache. What do you recommend?

Why don't you try Tylenol?

Three times a day.

That'll take about twenty minutes.

What's the prescription number?

Before you eat.

Role play

With another student, write and practice a conversation between a pharmacist and a customer. Order a prescription. Present your dialogue to the class.

16 Housing

Discuss

How many rooms do you have in your house?
What furniture do you have in your living room?
What appliances are there in your kitchen?
Do you like your apartment or house?

Listen, Read and Say

Landlord: This is the apartment for rent. It has four rooms. It has a living room, a dining room, a kitchen, and one bedroom.
Martin: Is the apartment furnished?
Landlord: Yes, the bedroom has a bed, but it doesn't have a dresser. The living room has a sofa and a chair.
Martin: That's great. How much is the rent?
Landlord: It's $800 a month.

Practice **Practice**

Practice this model with the rooms below.

The apartment has ___a kitchen___.

1. a kitchen

2. a dining room

3. a bedroom

4. a bathroom

5. a living room

62

complete

Write the names of the furniture on the items in each room.

Living Room

sofa
chair
TV set
coffee table
lamp
bookcase
wall-to-wall carpeting

Kitchen

refrigerator
stove
sink
cabinets
dishwasher
toaster
microwave
blender
table
chairs
counter

Bedroom

bed
chair
dresser
night table
lamp
rug
mirror

Practice this model. Talk about the furniture in this apartment.

| The _____bedroom_____ has _____a dresser_____. | The _____bedroom_____ doesn't have _____a night table_____. |

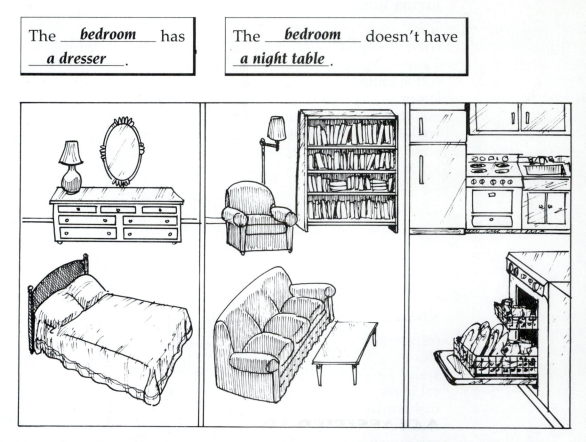

Complete these sentences about the furnished apartment above. Use has or doesn't have.

1. The bedroom _____*has*_____ a dresser.
2. The bedroom _____ a night table.
3. The bedroom _____ a mirror.
4. The living room _____ a TV set.
5. The living room _____ a bookcase.
6. The living room _____ a sofa.
7. The living room _____ wall-to-wall carpeting.
8. The kitchen _____ a stove.
9. The kitchen _____ a dishwasher.
10. The kitchen _____ a microwave.

Interaction

Talk to two students. Ask two students these questions about their apartment. Circle their answers in the chart below.

Do you have a _____?
Yes, I do.   *or*   No, I don't.

ITEM	STUDENT 1	STUDENT 2
a TV set	yes no	yes no
a stereo	yes no	yes no
a VCR	yes no	yes no
a microwave	yes no	yes no
a toaster oven	yes no	yes no
a blender	yes no	yes no
wall-to-wall carpeting	yes no	yes no
air conditioning	yes no	yes no
a CD player	yes no	yes no

A CLASSIFIED AD

BROOKLYN. State St. Furn 2 BR apt.
Modern ktchn. Heat incl. Avail immed.
$900/mo. 258-3126.

Putting It Together

Match these questions and answers about the classified ad above. Practice them with a partner.

How much is the rent?   It's in Brooklyn, on State Street.

Where is the apartment?   The heat is included, but not the
                                          gas and electric.
Are the utilities included?
                                          It's $900 a month.
How many bedrooms does it
  have?   Yes, it is.

When is the apartment available?   It has two.

Is the apartment furnished?   Immediately.

Role play

With another student, write and practice a conversation between a landlord and a person looking for an apartment. Ask for information about the apartment. Present your dialogue to the class.

17 Housing

Discuss

Do you live in a house or in an apartment?
Do you have a terrace or a back yard?
Where do you park?

Listen, Read and Say

Realtor: Hello.
George: I'm calling about the apartment for rent. Could you tell me about it?
Realtor: It's a two-bedroom apartment. The rent is $725 a month.
George: Does the apartment have air-conditioning?
Realtor: No, it doesn't.
George: Are the utilities included?
Realtor: The heat is included. You pay the electric.
George: I'd like to see the apartment.
Realtor: How's five o'clock tonight?
George: That's fine.

Practice Practice

Practice this model. Talk about the features in this apartment building.

The building has _a fire escape_.

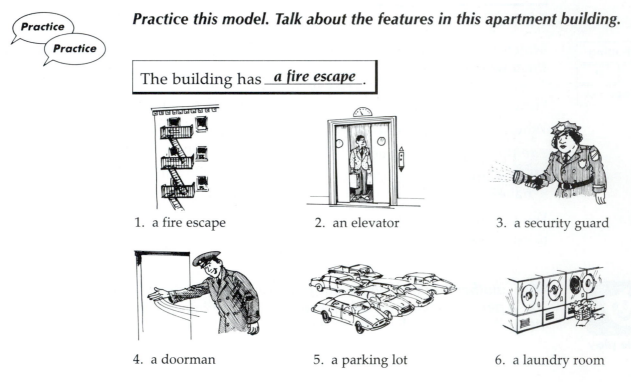

1. a fire escape

2. an elevator

3. a security guard

4. a doorman

5. a parking lot

6. a laundry room

Practice this model. Talk about the features in this apartment

The apartment has ___*air-conditioning*___.

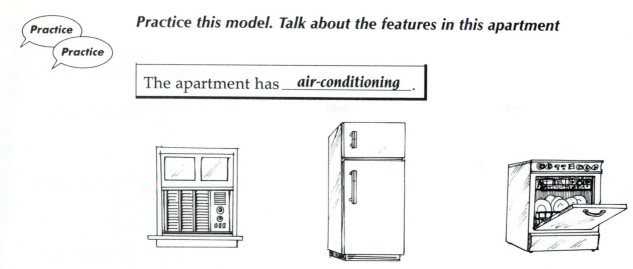

1. air-conditioning

2. a refrigerator

3. a dishwasher

4. wall-to-wall carpeting

5. a washer and dryer

6. a fireplace

complete

Answer these questions about your house or apartment. Use Yes, it does. or No, it doesn't.

1. Does your building have an elevator? _____

2. Does your building have a laundry room? _____

3. Does your building have a parking lot? _____

4. Does your building have a security guard? _____

5. Does your building have a fire escape? _____

6. Does your apartment have wall-to-wall carpeting? _____

7. Does your apartment have air-conditioning? _____

8. Does your apartment have a washer and dryer? _____

9. Does your apartment have a microwave? _____

10. Does your apartment have a dishwasher? _____

**Partner
Exercise**

Ask and answer questions about these apartments.

Student 1	Student 2
the building / an elevator?	*Listen carefully and help Student 1.*
Does the building have an elevator?	

Student 1

1. the building / an elevator?

2. Yes

3. the apartment / a terrace?

4. No

5. the building / a laundry room?

6. No

7. the apartment / a dishwasher?

8. Yes

9. the building / a fire escape?

10. Yes

(FOLD HERE)

Student 2
Listen carefully and help Student 1.

1. Does the building have an elevator?

2. Yes, it does.

3. Does the apartment have a terrace?

4. No, it doesn't.

5. Does the building have a laundry room?

6. No, it doesn't.

7. Does the apartment have a dishwasher?

8. Yes, it does.

9. Does the building have a fire escape?

10. Yes, it does.

Interaction

Ask two students these questions about their apartments or houses. Circle their answers in the chart below.

Does your apartment have _____?

or

Do you have a _____ in your apartment?

FEATURES	STUDENT 1	STUDENT 2
a fireplace	Yes No	Yes No
air-conditioning	Yes No	Yes No
a washer and dryer	Yes No	Yes No
a microwave	Yes No	Yes No
wall-to-wall carpeting	Yes No	Yes No
a fire escape	Yes No	Yes No
a back yard	Yes No	Yes No
an elevator	Yes No	Yes No
a laundry room	Yes No	Yes No

A CLASSIFIED AD

Putting It Together

Match these abbreviations with their meanings.

furn ———— utilities are included

h/hw ————— furnished

util incl   wall-to-wall carpeting

sec dep   air-conditioning

w/w   heat and hot water are included

ref   near

a/c   security deposit is required

nr   references are required

br   modern

lndry rm   bedroom

mod   laundry room

Talk about these ads for apartments for rent. Answer the questions about each apartment.

CORTLAND 1 BR off st prking a/c w/w util not incl. $650/mo. Call 237-8659

LOCKPORT 116 Ana St. 2 BR nr trans. $900/mo. sec dep. See super or call 391-9358

MAPLE PARK Furn 2 BR Immed occup. lndry rm in bldg. $800 mo. incl h/hw. 1 1/2 mo. sec dep. 965-3951

ROSELLE 4 rms. Mod ktch. w/w a/c. Walk to train. $700 mo. all util incl. Sec dep & ref req. 994-8735

1. Where is the apartment?
2. How many bedrooms does it have?
3. Are the utilities included?
4. Does the apartment have air-conditioning?
5. Does the apartment have wall-to-wall carpeting?
6. Does it have a parking lot?
7. Is the apartment furnished?
8. How much is the rent?
9. Is a security deposit required?
10. Are references required?

Role play

Bring in a classified ad for an apartment in your area. With another student, write a few sentences about the information in the ad. Present the information about the apartment to the class.

18 Work

Discuss

Where do you work?
What do you do?
What hours do you work?

Listen, Read and Say

Oscar: Liz, where do you work?
Liz: I work at United National Bank.
Oscar: Really? What do you do?
Liz: I'm a teller.
Oscar: What are your hours?
Liz: I work from 8:30 to 4:30.

Practice
Practice

Practice this model with the occupations below.

| I work at ___ *City Bank* ___. |
| I'm a/an ___ *teller* ___. |

| They work at ___ *Arco Corporation* ___. |
| They're ___ *machine operators* ___. |

1. I/City Bank
   teller

2. They/Arco Corporation
   machine operators

3. I/Simmons
   electrician

4. They/Bam Manufacturing
   secretaries

5. They/City Hospital
   nurses

6. I/Lincoln High School
   teacher

Practice this model with the occupations below.

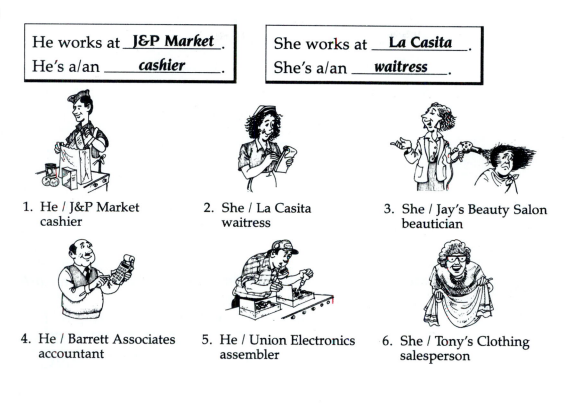

| He works at __J&P Market__. | She works at __La Casita__. |
| He's a/an ____cashier____. | She's a/an ____waitress____. |

1. He / J&P Market
   cashier

2. She / La Casita
   waitress

3. She / Jay's Beauty Salon
   beautician

4. He / Barrett Associates
   accountant

5. He / Union Electronics
   assembler

6. She / Tony's Clothing
   salesperson

**Partner
Exercise**

Talk about these occupations.

Student 1 I / at Bam Manufacturing I work at Bam Manufacturing.	**Student 2** *Listen carefully and help Student 1.*
1. I / at Bam Manufacturing	1. I work at Bam Manufacturing.
2. I / a machine operator	2. I'm a machine operator.
3. He / at Central Hospital	3. He works at Central Hospital.
4. He / a nurse	4. He's a nurse.
5. She / at LMK Electronics	5. She works at LMK Electronics.
6. She / an assembler	6. She's an assembler.
7. They / at U&B Corporation	7. They work at U&B Corporation.
8. They / secretaries	8. They're secretaries.
9. He / at R&K Construction	9. He works at R&K Construction.
10. He / a plumber	10. He's a plumber.
11. I / at _____	11. I work at _____.
12. I / a _____	12. I'm a _____.

(FOLD HERE)

CONCEN TRATION

Cut out and play the Concentration Game on page 97. Match each work picture with the correct sentence.

Complete these sentences.

1. I ___**work at**___ Arco Corporation.
2. I _**'m a**_____ machine operator.
3. They _____ General Hospital.
4. They _____ nurses.
5. She _____ United Bank.
6. She _____ supervisor.
7. He _____ Union Electronics.
8. He _____ assembler.
9. They _____ Oakland Elementary School.
10. They _____ teachers.

Practice

Practice

Practice this model. Talk about the hours these people work.

Howard works the first shift from 7:30 a.m. to 3:30 p.m.

SIMON MANUFACTURING

Howard	1st shift	7:30 a.m. to 3:30 p.m.
Ellen	2nd shift	3:30 p.m. to 11:30 p.m.
Gary and Sue	3rd shift	11:30 p.m. to 7:30 a.m.

GENERAL HOSPITAL

Jill	1st shift	7:00 a.m. to 3:00 p.m.
Peter and Mark	2nd shift	3:00 p.m. to 11:00 p.m.
David	3rd shift	11:00 p.m. to 7:00 a.m.

Ask three students these questions about their jobs. Fill in their answers in the chart below.

Where do you work?   What do you do?   What hours do you work?

Interaction

STUDENT	PLACE	JOB	HOURS

CLASSIFIED JOB ADS

Putting It Together

Match these abbreviations with their meanings.

p/t   required

f/t   preferred

req   part-time

exp   references

pref   full-time

ref   benefits

bnfts   experience

Talk about these classified job ads. Answer the questions below about each job.

> AUTO MECHANIC exp with brakes, mufflers, tune-ups & general repairs. FT days. $12/hr starting. Call Mike 968-3414.

> DENTAL ASSISTANT PT Private dental practice, flexible hours. Exp pref. X-ray license req. Call 355-3050 to apply.

> DRIVERS—LIMOUSINE Large busy car service is seeking FT and PT drivers. All hours available. Must have clean license. Earn up to $450/wk. Call George 429-8372.

> OFFICE SECRETARY FT eves. Mature person to work in pleasant office. Phone and typing skills (40-50 wpm). Salary based on exp. Exc. benefits. Send resume to Clinton Corp 55 Summer Ave Newark, NJ 07102.

1. What's the position?
2. What are the job responsibilities?
3. Are there any benefits? What are they?
4. What's the salary?
5. Is experience necessary?
6. What are the hours?
7. Is the job full-time or part-time?
8. What are the requirements?
9. Are references required?
10. How do you apply for this position?

Role play

Bring in a few classified ads for jobs in your area. With another student, write a few sentences about the information in the ad. Present the information about the job to the class.

19 Jms

Discuss

How do you like your job?
What do you like about your job?
What don't you like about your job?
What are your benefits?

Listen, Read and Say

George: How do you like your job?
 Pierre: I like it. It's interesting.
  How about you?
George: I don't like my job because
  the pay is low.

Practice Practice

Practice this model with the reasons below.

| I like my job because ***the pay is good*** . | He likes his job because ***the pay is good*** . |

1. the pay is good

2. the work is interesting

3. the work is light

4. the hours are good

5. the boss is friendly

6. the benefits are good

Practice this model with the reasons below.

Practice / Practice

| I don't like my job because **the pay is low**. | He doesn't like his job because **the pay is low**. |

1. the pay is low

2. the work is boring

3. the work is heavy

4. the hours are bad

5. the boss is unfriendly

6. the benefits aren't good

Partner Exercise

Talk about these jobs.

Student 1
I / like / hours
I like my hours.

1. I / like / hours
2. I / like / job
3. I / like / boss
4. He / like / job
5. He / like / hours
6. He / like / boss
7. She / like / boss
8. She / like / shift
9. She / like / hours
10. They / like / boss

(FOLD HERE)

Student 2
Listen carefully and help Student 1.

1. I like my hours.
2. I like my job.
3. I don't like my boss.
4. He likes his job.
5. He doesn't like his hours.
6. He likes his boss.
7. She likes her work.
8. She doesn't like her shift.
9. She doesn't like her hours.
10. They don't like the boss.

Complete these sentences about jobs.

1. I _____like my job_____ because the pay ___is___ good.
2. I _____ because the work _____ boring.
3. I _____ because the work _____ interesting.
4. She _____ because the benefits _____ good.
5. He _____ because the pay _____ low.
6. He _____ because the workers _____ friendly.
7. She _____ because the workload _____ heavy.
8. I _____ because the boss _____ unfriendly.
9. I _____ because the work _____ difficult.
10. She _____ because the workload _____ light.

Interaction

Ask three students these questions about their jobs. Fill in their answers in the chart below.

What do you do?
How do you like your job?
Why do you like it?   or
Why don't you like it?

STUDENT	JOB	OPINION	REASON
Maria	nurse's aide	(Like it) / Don't like it	benefits are good / boss is helpful
		Like it / Don't like it	
		Like it / Don't like it	
		Like it / Don't like it	

HOW DO YOU LIKE YOUR JOB?

Talk about Mark's job. What are his hours, his pay, his benefits? Why does he like his job? What doesn't he like about it?

Mark Drexel

Job:	bus driver
Hours:	6:00 a.m. to 3:00 p.m.
Salary:	$15 / hour
Benefits:	medical insurance, 10 days vacation, retirement plan
Pros:	hours / salary / benefits / interesting
Cons:	noise / air pollution / boss

Match these short conversations about work. Practice them with a partner.

How do you like your job?   I don't like her.

How's your salary?   They're good, especially the
                                              medical.

How's your boss?   I like it a lot.

How are your benefits?   It's good. I get a raise every
                                              year.

How do you like your hours?   The noise and the pollution
                                              are bad.

What don't you like about your job?   They're great for me because I
                                              like to get up early.

Complete this information about your own job.

Job: _____

Hours: _____

Benefits: _____

Pros: _____

Cons: _____

Role play

With another student, write and practice a conversation about your jobs. Talk about your work, hours, and benefits. Discuss why you like or don't like your jobs. Present your dialogue to the class.

20 Telephone

Discuss

Do you have a telephone at home?
Which room is it in?
Who do you call on the phone?
Who calls you?
How do you feel when you talk
   on the phone in English?

Listen, Read and Say

Mrs. Taylor: Hello.
     Kyoko: Hello. This is Kyoko Okamoto.
                Can I speak to Mrs. Taylor?
Mrs. Taylor: This is Mrs. Taylor.

Practice

Practice

Match each picture below with one of the sentences.

A. The phone is ringing.
B. He's picking up the receiver.
C. She's hanging up. He's hanging up.
D. He's dialing the telephone number.
E. They're talking on the phone.
F. She's picking up the receiver.

1. _____

2. _____

3. _____

4. _____

5. _____

6. _____

Practice calling another student in your class. Use your name and the name of another student in the class.

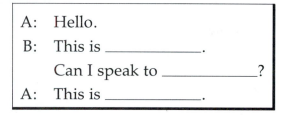

A: Hello.
B: This is _____.
   Can I speak to _____?
A: This is _____.

Practice calling another student in your class. A third person answers the phone. Use your name and the name of another student in the class.

A: Hello.
B: Hello. Can I please speak with _____?
A: Who's calling, please?
B: This is _____.
A: Hold on, please.

Interaction

Ask two students these questions about the kinds of telephone calls they make. Fill in their answers in the chart below.

CALLS	STUDENT 1		STUDENT 2	
Do you call the doctor?	yes	no	yes	no
Do you call work?	yes	no	yes	no
Do you call directory assistance?	yes	no	yes	no
Do you make appointments?	yes	no	yes	no
Do you make reservations?	yes	no	yes	no
Do you talk to friends?	yes	no	yes	no
Do you order pizza?	yes	no	yes	no
Do you call school?	yes	no	yes	no

DIRECTORY ASSISTANCE

Listen, Read and Say

Directory Assistance:	Operator 22. For what city?
Caller:	Detroit. I'd like the number of Ken Rogers on Central Avenue.
Directory Assistance:	Please hold for the number.
Computer:	The number is 568-7659, 568-7659.

Practice
Practice

Practice this model. Ask to speak to the people below. Give any telephone number.

> A: Operator 22. For what city?
> B: __*San Antonio*__ . I'd like the number of __*Charles Colon*__
> on __*Grove Street*__ .
> A: Please hold for the number. The number is __229-3158__ .

CITY	PERSON	ADDRESS
San Antonio	Charles Colon	Grove Street
Philadelphia	Sandra Farino	23rd Street
Chicago	Richard Diego	Washington Boulevard
Dallas	Diana Tran	Rodeo Drive
Seattle	Andrew Miller	Tice Place
Miami	Judy Kennedy	15th Street

Match these short conversations on a telephone. Practice them with a partner.

Can I speak to Jim Gibson?	This is Mr. Cruz.
Can I speak to Mr. Cruz?	She's not here right now.
Can I speak to Marian?	Speaking.
Is Paula there?	This is Terry.
Who's calling, please?	Hold on, please.

TELEPHONE DIRECTORY

Putting It Together

Find these telephone numbers on the telephone page below.

Dennis Brooks	_____	Pamela Brooks	_____
Sarah Bronson	_____	Oliver Brown	_____
Joshua Brody	_____	Irving Bross	_____
Ralph Brown	_____	Russell Brown	_____
Robert Brown (York)	_____	Helen Brody	_____

---

30   Brody—Browne

Brody F 400 Embry Dr. Blmfld	755-8574	Brown C T 203 Lyde Pl. Davis	494-7392
Brody H 2114 Oak St. Newton	689-3929	Brown Charles E 93 Forest Av. Blmfld	755-8293
Brody Joshua 2062 Miller A. Newton	689-2297	Brown Chas A 19 Boynton Av. Blmfld	755-9394
Brody M 32 Sandra Circle York	514-7798	Brown David 234 Eton Pl. York	514-5383
Brody Marc 392 Parkview Ave. York	514-2947	Brown Donald 920 North Av. York	514-3709
Brody Paul 34 Broad St. Blmfld	755-9034	Brown Duane 24 Sunnywood Dr. Blmfld	755-5152
Brody Paul 34 Broad St. Blmfld	755-9783	Brown Francis D 195 E 2nd St. Davis	494-9080
Brody R 63 River Dr. York	514-8201	Brown G 239 Richmond Davis	494-7156
Brody Robert 194 North A. Newton	689-2398	Brown G R 867 Westfield Av. York	514-7922
Brody Roger 33 Fox St. Davis	494-8833	Brown George 52 Cooper Rd. Newton	689-8240
Brogly G F 1180 Ridge Drive Blmfld	755-8096	Brown George L 23 Essex Rd. Davis	494-1127
Brois S J 773 Lamberts Rd. Blmfld	755-3955	Brown H 2216 River Dr. Davis	494-6614
Brois V M 54 Wells A. York	514-0902	Brown H. 70 Montrose Av. York	514-9875
Bronski John A 2245 First A. Davis	494-3997	Brown Ira 815 Bridge St. Blmfld	755-8227
Bronson S J 295 Bridle Path York	514-3984	Brown J B Mrs 33 Valley Rd. Davis	494-3822
Bronston J 15 N Elm Blmfld	755-3844	Brown Jas B 408 South Av. York	514-3224
Brookside Research & Management Co	755-8200	Brown Jody R 2061 Mountain Av. Davis	494-4494
785 Broad St. Blmfld		Brown Kenneth 921 Penn Av. Blmfld	755-5947
Brookman P Rbt 654 Ocean Dr. York	514-3298	Brown Kevin 310 Montague Av Davis	494-4494
Brooks A A 428 Summit Av. Newton	689-4932	Brown Lrry 20 Essex Rd. Davis	494-9661
Brooks David 259 Emmets York	514-7745	Brown Leon 13 Johnson Pl. Davis	494-9617
Brooks Dennis 127 Oak Blmfld	755-3771	Brown M 1305 Boulevard Blmfld	755-9197
Brooks Louise 122 US Hwy 41 Newton	689-0908	Brown Natalie 547 E Broad St. Blmfld	755-1132
Brooks Murphy & Co CPAs 1122 US Hwy	689-0903	Brown Neil W 33 Elmer St. Blmfld	755-1224
41 Newton		Brown Noel 265 Prospect Av. Blmfld	755-5458
Brooks Pamela 167 Cooper Rd. Davis	494-3387	Brown Oliver MD 523 North Av. York	514-4344
Brooks Robt 141 Olive St. Blmfld	755-4501	Brown Paul DDS 223 Summit Av. Davis	494-1703
Brooks Lawn & Garden 890 US Hwy 41	689-3372	Brown Paul 207 Grand St. Davis	494-8323
Newton		Brown Peter 107 Oak St. Davis	494-3906
Brooks W 444 Myrtle St. Davis	494-6711	Brown Philip 627 Hillcrest Rd. Blmfld	755-1523
Brookside Church 67 Richards St. Newton	689-9090	Brown Philip 104 Willow St. Blmfld	755-8933
Brosman R 103 Martine A. Blmfld	755-7765	Brown Quentin 127 Sylvan La. Davis	494-8767
Bross Irving 338 Short Dr. Blmfld	755-0317	Brown R N 133 Woodland Av. York	514-6153
Brostek M 532 Coles Pl. Blmfld	755-4583	Brown Ralph A 754 River St. Blmfld	755-4033
Brotman David and Lynne 710 Emery	755-6747	Brown Regina 44 Oakland Av. Blmfld	755-5054
Way Blmfld		Brown Richard W 55 Alden Av. Blmfld	755-1182
Brotman L 432 Pecos Way Blmfld	755-3925	Brown Robert 201 Downer Av. Blmfld	755-5041
Brower Lucille 35 Scudder Rd. Blfld	755-0316	Brown Robt 520 Ripley Av. Davis	494-2195
Brower Melvin C 155 King St. York	514-5839	Brown Robt G 433 Center St. York	514-3398
Brower W D 748 Boulevard Blmfld	755-4829	Brown Roger 340 Coles Av. Davis	494-8861
Brown Arden 7838 Fairacres Av. York	514-5723	Brown Russel W 518 Birch St. Blmfld	755-5501
Brown B 466 Broad St. Blmfld	755-0482	Brown Stanley 83 Second St. Davis	494-0711
Brown C 483 John St. Davis	494-5484		

Role play

With another student, write and practice two telephone calls. First, call and ask to speak to a friend. Second, call directory assistance and ask for a telephone number. Present one of your dialogues to the class.

Concentration Games

		He's from Colombia.
		She's from Mexico.
		They're from Japan.
		They're from Poland.
		He's from Haiti.
		They're from Puerto Rico.
		He's from Egypt.
		She's from Portugal.

UNIT 4 ■ YOUR ADDRESS

thirteen	fourteen	13	14
fifteen	sixteen	15	16
twelve	twenty	12	20
thirty	forty	30	40
fifty	sixty	50	60

UNIT 7 ■ TRANSPORTATION

$4.25	four dollars and twenty-five cents
$4.50	four dollars and fifty cents
$13.75	thirteen dollars and seventy-five cents
$30.75	thirty dollars and seventy-five cents
$14.25	fourteen dollars and twenty-five cents
$40.25	forty dollars and twenty-five cents
$16.50	sixteen dollars and fifty cents
$60.75	sixty dollars and seventy-five cents

		It's next to the bank.
		It's between the bank and the police station.
		It's across from the movie theater.
		It's between the library and the hospital.
		It's across from the fire station.
		It's next to the hospital.
		It's across from the employment office.
		It's next to the Post Office.

UNIT 9 ■ COMMUNITY RESOURCES

		He's looking for a book.
		She's returning some books.
		She's paying her taxes.
		She's depositing some money.
		He's cashing his check.
		He's buying some stamps.
		They're mailing some letters.
		They're sending packages.

UNIT 10 ■ SUPERMARKET

			Where are the oranges? Where's the spaghetti? Where are the napkins?
			Where's the bread? Where's the oil? Where are the rolls?
			Where are the onions? Where's the flour? Where are the bananas?

UNIT 12 ■ CLOTHES

		I'm looking for a pair of gloves. I'm looking for a suit.
		I'm looking for a bathing suit. I'm looking for a skirt.
		I'm looking for a pair of socks. I'm looking for a pair of boots.
		I'm looking for a sweater. I'm looking for a pair of pajamas.

		How much is this bathrobe?
		How much are these shorts?
		How much are these running shoes?
		How much is this slip?
$27.		How much is this scarf?
	$24	How much is this turtleneck?
$55		How much are these earrings?
	$18	How much are these sunglasses?

I	*I*	I have a headache. I have a stomachache.
I	*I*	I have a toothache. I have an earache.
he	*he*	He has a fever. He has a cough.
she	*he*	She has a cold. He has a sore throat.

UNIT 18 ■ WORK

I / bank	they / factory	I work at a bank. They work at a factory.
they / hospital	I / high school	They work at a hospital. I work at a high school.
she / restaurant	he / store	She works at a restaurant. He works at a store.
she / beauty parlor	he / factory	She works at a beauty parlor. He works at a factory.